TORAH and YOU

PART ONE

TORAH and YOU

A Value Clarification Text

YOU

PART ONE

stories by	**Ruth Samuels**
Value Clarification exercises by	**Sol Scharfstein**
art by	**Arthur Friedman**

KTAV PUBLISHING HOUSE

Table of Contents

Torah and You

JEWISH HISTORY TELLS us that the Torah was given to the Jewish people more than 5,000 years ago. It is our special treasure. Since that time our ancestors, no matter which country they lived in, have been studying the Torah and learning and living its lessons.

The Torah is the foundation stone of the Jewish religion. It contains our beginning history, the laws of Judaism, and lessons about right and wrong.

In the Torah you will find exciting stories about your ancestors, Adam and Eve, Noah, Abraham, Isaac, Jacob, Sarah, Rebecca, Leah, Joseph, Aaron, Moses, and Joshua.

Sometimes the Torah was hard to understand. Then, the Rabbis would try to make it easier and more meaningful. Some Rabbis made up stories called Midrashim. These stories help explain what the Rabbis thought the Torah meant.

Other Rabbis had a different way of explaining the meaning of the Torah. These Rabbis asked questions and then answered them. Sometimes the questions and answers were about the story, sometimes about the world your ancestors lived in, and sometimes about how to know what was right and wrong.

The Rabbis recognized that the Torah has many messages about understanding ourselves and how we act towards other people. Some of the Torah ideas are easy to find, and some are hidden and more difficult to find. So, they said, *Hafoch ba, hafoch ba, dekulai ba* ("Turn it, turn it, everything is in it").

It doesn't make any difference how old you are — just read the Torah stories and search, and you will find their hidden treasures.

The Why and Because section is a search-and-find treasure hunt that discovers important ideas in the Torah story.

Later on, as you become a more experienced Torah scholar, you will be able to *hafoch ba* ("Turn it ") and ask your own questions and find your own answers.

As you go through life you will meet all kinds of people and experience different situations. You will have to make choices between what is right and what is wrong, what is true and what is false, what is good and what is bad, what is beautiful and what is ugly, what is Jewish and what is not.

Out of these experiences and choices you will grow and you will learn. The choices will be a guide to your life. These choices are called values.

These Value Clarification exercises will help you apply the message of the Torah to your everyday life, to your family, to your friends, and to your neighbors. In this section you will learn about respecting others, helping people, making decisions, brotherhood, friendship, language, charity, etc.

Sometimes the questions in these exercises are tough, and sometimes there are no "correct" answers. In that case, answer as best as you can or discuss the problem with your teacher, classmates, or your parents.

There are also Value Clarification exercises about famous people. The biographies are about people who made the world better, or helped the Jewish community. By reading about these people you can learn how to make your own life and your career more meaningful.

The lessons of the Torah are timeless. Even today, the Torah helps us understand ourselves and teaches us how to live honestly, peacefully, and happily.

I hope you enjoy studying *Torah and You. Torah and You* will help you learn a lot about yourself, and help make you into a more caring and better person.

Hafoch ba, hafoch ba, dekulai ba!

How God Made The World

BEFORE THE BEGINNING there were no birds to sing, no flowers to smell, no sun to give light. Everything was dark and empty. But ... God was there.

And God said, "Let there be light," and there was light. And God called the light "Day" and the dark "Night." And that was the very first day in the world.

On the second day God divided the world into two parts. The upper half was the sky and the air, which has spread over the earth like a tent. The lower half of the world was below the sky and that was a mass of dark water.

On the third day, God separated the waters from the dry land and called the dry land "Earth." The waters became mighty oceans and rivers and brooks and waterfalls. Now the ground was ready for trees, flowers and grass, so God made them next. There were red, red roses, yellow daffodils, purple asters, orange sunflowers, and blue forget-me-nots. God made the tall trees and gave the world all kinds of food for the people who were going to live there.

On the fourth day, God made the world even more beautiful. On the fourth day God created the sun and the moon and the twinkling stars. The sun to give light and warmth to the earth by day, and the moon to give a soft restful light at night. The stars seemed to sparkle and when God looked at the stars they seemed to be laughing with joy. God smiled, and was happy because the world was good.

On the fifth day, God put the first living creatures upon the earth. The oceans, the rivers and the brooks were filled with all kinds of wonderful fish, in all shapes and sizes, from the huge whale to the tiny minnow.

And the air was filled with beautiful birds of all kinds and all colors: red birds, and bluebirds and friendly robins. The world was filled with color and music, as the beautiful fish swam through the clear waters and the birds sang their lovely songs.

On the sixth day God made the animals of the earth, the gentle cows, woolie sheep, huge elephants and furry kittens. All the animals loved each other: the graceful and gentle deer were not afraid of the fierce wolves and tigers. Everyone lived in peace. And once more God looked about and saw that the world was good. On the sixth day God also made the first man who ever lived. God called this man, Adam.

CHOOSE THE CORRECT ANSWER.

1. Everything was dark and empty but _____ was there.
   a. God
   b. the President
   c. Moses

2. On the third day God separated the waters from the dry land and called the dry land _____.
   a. earth
   b. sky
   c. river

3. On the fifth day, God put the first living _____ upon the earth.
   a. creatures
   b. automobiles
   c. rocket ships

4. All the animals _____ each other.
   a. loved
   b. hated
   c. blessed

DAYS OF CREATION. MATCH THE COLUMNS.

A	B
1. On the first day God created	sun, moon, and stars
2. On the second day God created	animals and man
3. On the third day God created	fish and birds
4. On the fourth day God created	light
5. On the fifth day God created	sky and water
6. On the sixth day God created	earth, flowers, and trees

WHY did God create Adam last of all?

BECAUSE it was God's plan to complete the world so that humans could live in it.

Now there was earth to grow food for them and air for them to breathe. The sun lighted and warmed the earth by day, and the moon and stars lighted the world at night. There was cool, delicious water to drink and delicious fruits and vegetables to eat. The animals provided skins and wool to keep them warm.

On the sixth day all was now ready for the first man and woman. Now they could live and enjoy God's wonderful new world.

YOU ARE SPECIAL

The Torah tells us that God created the world in six days. The world was a planet with pure air and clean water. The earth was carpeted with trees, grass, and herbs.

All kinds of animals playfully jumped and ran and crawled through the forests and jungles.

The sky was alive with singing birds, soaring through the air. Wondrous fishes in all shapes and colors tumbled and swam through the pure clean waters.

Everything in God's world was in place for the first man and woman.

The Torah tells us that people are special. God created the world and gave humans special powers to make it a happier and a better place in which to live.

God gave humans brains that can write books, invent machines, paint pictures, build airplanes, cure diseases, tell jokes, and sing songs.

You too can help make the world healthier, better, and happier.

1. Name a new machine or medicine you would like to see someone invent.

The magical care. It's a medicine that cures everything.

2. How will it make the world happier, better, or healthier?

No one will be sick.

3. Name something you would like to learn to do.

4. How will you go about learning it?

5. How will it make you a better person?

Adam and Eve

IT WAS NOW the sixth day of creation. It was a wonderful, light, and joyful world. The earth was carpeted with green grass, tall trees and colorful flowers. The jungles, forests, and meadows were alive with playful animals. Singing birds soared through the skies and rested in the trees that God had made. The mighty oceans, wavy seas and softly murmuring brooks were filled with swiftly swimming fish.

The sun, moon and stars smiled on the peaceful world. God had created it all in six days and it was very good.

Now, on the sixth day God decided to create another creature to enjoy the world and take care of it.

So, God formed the first man from the dust of the earth. This man had strong arms and legs and a brain to think with and plan and choose and create. God breathed the breath of life into the first man and he became a living creature.

God said, "I will call you Adam, because you were created from the **adamah** (hebrew for earth)".

God planted Adam a beautiful garden, filled with trees and flowers and animals and running water. This special place was called the Garden of Eden.

That day, God walked with Adam in the Garden of Eden. And God said, "Adam you will rule this world and all that I have created. This is now your world. Since you will rule over all my creatures you must give them special names."

So Adam gave names to all the fish in the water, animals on the land and birds in the sky.

All the creatures in the world had mates, but Adam was alone. Poor Adam, he was very sad and lonely.

God decided to give Adam one more special gift. God caused Adam to fall into a deep sleep. Gently, God took a rib from Adam's side and made it into a beautiful woman.

Adam called this first woman Eve. Adam and Eve lived happily in the Garden of Eden.

On the sixth day God ended his work of creation. The world was now warmed by the sun and slept under the moon and stars. The world was alive and at peace. God was very happy.

On the seventh day God rested from his work. God blessed the seventh day in a special way. And God called the seventh day "Shabbat."

"For ever afterward, it will be good for humans to follow my example," God said. "All people should work for six days and set aside the Shabbat for a day of rest and prayer."

9

CHOOSE THE CORRECT ANSWER.

1. All people should work for six days and set aside the _____ for a day of rest and prayer.

a. Shabbat

b. New Year

c. Hanukah

2. So, God formed the first man from the _____ of the earth.

a. dust

b. rocks

c. water

3. God breathed the breath of _____ into the first man.

a. life

b. death

c. wine

4. "I will call you Adam, because you were created from _____."

a. wood

b. iron

c. adamah

5. God called the first woman _____.

a. Judy

b. Adam

c. Eve

MATCH THE COLUMNS.

A	B
1. Adam and	day of rest
2. Garden of	world
3. Shabbat	Eve
4. God created the	stars
5. Sun, moon, and	Eden

WHY did God create Adam from the dust of the earth?

BECAUSE God wanted to show the world that all human beings are equal. Our Rabbis say that God took all colors of dust from the four corners of the earth, north, east, west, and south, and formed it into a human.

In this way no person, or group of people, can say, "Adam was created from our earth and therefore we are greater than all other people."

Every person then, no matter what his race, color, or religion, is equal. Every person in the world is descended from Adam and Eve.

10

WE ARE ALL ONE PEOPLEHOOD

The Torah tells us that we are all members of one human family—one peoplehood.

Every person, no matter the race, color, or religion, is equal. Everyone is just as important as you are. That's what peoplehood means.

We are all one peoplehood. This means you should be fair to all people even if they are different. They may be a different color, speak a different language, pray differently, wear different clothes, but they are all God's people.

In many ways we are all alike. In many ways we have lots of differences. Sometimes these differences can be frightening. This is especially so if we don't understand and are not used to seeing strange differences.

Draw a picture of someone you like.

Draw a picture of someone you do not like or are afraid of.

1. How is the person you like the same as you? How is that person different? _____

_____

2. How is the person you do not like or are afraid of the same as you? How is that person different? _____

_____

3. What is different about the person you do not like or are afraid of? ____

_____

Cain and Abel

AFTER ADAM AND Eve left the Garden of Eden, God sent them two healthy sons, called Cain and Abel.

Adam and Eve watched their sons grow up to be fine, strong men. Adam taught Cain how to plough the ground and plant seeds and raise fruits and vegetables. He taught Abel how to care for sheep.

But though Cain and Abel were both strong and healthy, there was one great difference between them. Cain did not like his work. It made him angry when he had to dig hard in the soil. He hated carrying the heavy sacks of grain, and the baskets of fruits and vegetables at harvest time. Cain grumbled and complained all the time he worked.

But Abel loved his work. He loved every sheep in this flock, and when the little lambs were born, Abel cared for them tenderly. He never forgot to thank God for blessing him with so many fine, fat sheep.

One day, Abel looked at all his fine sheep and said:

"God has been very good to me. I must offer the Lord a gift."

Cain also decided to sacrifice to God. When Cain arrived at the place where the sacrifices were made, he found Abel already there with his fine fat lamb.

"What are you doing here?" asked Cain.

"I think it is only fair that I give back a part of what God has given me," answered his brother.

Then Abel noticed that Cain was holding something behind his back.

"What is that you are carrying?" he asked.

Cain's face became very red as he brought forth the basket of withered fruits and vegetables for Abel to see Abel tried to admire the poor offering, because he did not want to hurt Cain's feelings.

But suddenly, as Cain looked at Abel's fat little lamb, and then at his own poor offering, he was so ashamed that he flung his basket to the ground.

Cain became so angry that he picked up a stone and threw it with all his might at his brother, hitting him with the stone. Abel gave him one startled glance, then fell to the ground.

Cain was frightened at what he had done. He was no longer angry, only sorry. He ran to Abel and knelt on the ground beside him, sobbing:

"What have I done! I have killed my own brother!"

Then he quickly buried Abel's body. But when he had finished, he heard a mighty voice crying:

"Where is Abel, your brother?"

Cain trembled, for he knew this was the voice of God.

"I do not know," Cain answered. "Am I my brother's keeper?"

God's voice became very stern, and he cried:

"You have spilled your brother's blood into the earth. No more will the earth give you fruits and vegetables and grain! You must wander from place to place from this day on!"

And Cain said to the Lord, "My punishment is greater than I can bear. You have driven me out from among men. If any man finds me, he will kill me, because I shall be alone, and no one will be my friend."

But God put a mark upon Cain's forehead so that no harm would come to him, and then told him he must begin his weary wandering from place to place, never resting.

CHOOSE THE CORRECT ANSWER.

1. God sent Adam and Eve two fine sons, Cain and _____.

    a. Susan

    b. Harry

    (c.) Abel

2. Adam taught Cain how to raise _____.

    a. fruits and vegetables

    (b.) cows and sheep

    c. chutes and ladders

3. "God has been very good to me. I must offer the _____ a gift."

    (a.) Lord

    b. captain

    c. general

4. "Am I my _____ keeper?"

    (a.) brother's

    b. sister's

    c. uncle's

MATCH THE COLUMNS. WHO AM I?

1. I am the first person in the world.   Abel

2. I am the first woman in the world.   Adam

3. I killed my brother.   Eve

4. My brother killed me.   Cain

WHY did God punish Cain by putting a mark upon his forehead?

BECAUSE Cain was like a murderer on a wanted list. He lived in fear and was frightened by the terrible crime he had committed.

When God saw the suffering and sorrow of Cain, God decided that Cain had paid for his crime. So God showed mercy to this unhappy, homeless man. He accepted Cain's plea for forgiveness. God put a mark upon Cain's forehead so that all who met him would know that he had paid for his crime.

Cain was now left in peace to wander the face of the earth.

WHAT WOULD YOU DO?

The Torah tells us that Cain was the first murderer in the world. Cain realized that he had committed a great wrong. But Cain could not undo his mistake and bring his brother back to life. So God punished him and made him a homeless wanderer.

None of us are perfect, and sometimes we make mistakes. When we do the wrong thing, we can be sorry and try to correct it.

Sometimes, all you have to do is to say "I'm sorry." Then the person you have hurt feels better, and you do too. But sometimes it is not so simple, and you have to fix or make up for the wrong things you have done.

1. **Your friend asks for help with the homework. You refuse and your friend fails the test.**

   How would you make up with your friend? _____

   _____

2. **You borrow a record from your friend without telling him and you lose it.**

   What would you do? _____

   _____

3. **Your parents depend upon you to do something special around the house. You are so busy having fun that you don't do it.**

   How would you make up to your parents? _____

   _____

4. **You become so angry that you smack your brother or sister.**

   How would you go about making up? _____

   _____

The First Rainbow

ALL THE EARTH was filled with the family of Adam and Eve. But it was not a happy world. Men and women stole from each other. Children disobeyed their parents. Sometimes wicked people even killed each other.

God saw all the wickedness and was very sad. God was pleased, however, that there was at least one man who was good and kind. That man was Noah. Even though Noah lived in the midst of wicked people, he did not allow their stupidity to turn him from his good ways. One day, God spoke to Noah and said:

"I am going to send a great rain to the earth, because the people are very wicked. You must build a big boat so you and your family will not drown.

Noah thanked God, and then went to tell his three sons, Shem, Ham and Japeth that he was going to build an ark and they must help him.

One of his sons said to his brother, "Do you suppose that our father is getting so old that he doesn't know what he is doing? Where is this ark to sail when it is built? Across the fields on the waves of grain?"

But his brother shook his head and answered,

"Our father has never commanded us to do anything wrong. He is very wise and good. Therefore, let us help him build his ark as we should."

And Noah did what God told him to do, although it must have seemed very strange to all the people around to see them build this great ark where there was no water for it to sail upon. It was a long time that Noah and his sons

were at work building the ark, while the wicked people around wondered and laughed at Noah for building a great ship where there was no sea.

When the ark was finished, God said to Noah:

"Take two of all the animals of the earth into the ark."

And then it began to rain.

It rained for forty days and forty nights. Soon the world was covered with water. Noah's ark rocked back and forth on the waves like a toy, but everyone inside was safe and dry.

Then one day, the rain stopped. The Ark landed on Mt. Ararat. The sun came out and the waters were dried up. God told Noah to let the animals go out of the Ark. The birds flew away to the tree tops. The elephants and giraffes and kangaroos went back to the forest.

"We must thank God for saving us," said Noah. He took some stones and built an altar. Then he put gifts on the altar and bowed to say a "thank you" prayer.

God was pleased with Noah.

"Noah," said God, "look up in the sky. What you see there is my promise to you that I will never send a flood again to cover the earth."

When Noah looked up, he saw a wide band of beautiful colors that stretched clear across the sky. It was the first rainbow! Then God said:

"Whenever you see a rainbow in the sky, remember that I am here. I will never again send the flood to destroy the earth. I always keep my promise."

"I always keep my promise."

CHOOSE THE CORRECT ANSWER.

1. God decided to destroy the world because _____.

    a. it was wicked

    b. it was a happy place

    c. there were too many people

2. Noah was saved from the flood because he was _____.

    a. good and kind

    b. rich

    c. a good actor

3. It rained for _____.

    a. two weeks

    b. one whole year

    c. forty days and forty nights

4. After the flood the Ark came to rest _____.

    a. on Mount Ararat

    b. in the garden of Eden

    c. in Jerusalem

MATCH THE COLUMNS.

A	B
1. Noah's	Ararat
2. forty days and	good and kind
3. Mount	ark
4. Shem, Ham, and	forty nights
5. Noah	Japeth

WHY did God place a rainbow in the sky?
BECAUSE God wanted to show the people a sign that never again would the world be flooded.

    The rain is over and the warm sun breaks through the dark clouds. Suddenly a dazzling band of colors arcs across the sky. The rainbow hugs the earth like a parent hugging a child. Saying, "Yes, I will never again punish My children by flooding the earth."

THE MITZVAH OF TZEDAKAH

Back in Noah's day, people felt a need to thank God. They took the best of their animals or crops, placed them on an altar (*mizbeyakh*), and burned them as an offering to show their devotion to God. By giving up something of value, they not only showed their love and respect, but also their trust that God would help them to prosper and replace those possessions.

Today we have other ways of showing our thanks to God. We can do our best to observe the laws of the Torah, to do mitzvot (like giving Tzedakah and being kind to others), and of course we pray to God, telling our feelings directly.

You can do the mitzvah of Tzedakah by giving money, sharing your things, and giving your time and work.

How would you perform the mitzvah of Tzedakah in these cases? Think of examples.

1. Giving money

   Example: _____

   _____

   _____

2. Giving your time and work

   Example: _____

   _____

   _____

3. Sharing your things

   Example: _____

   _____

Tower of Babel

AFTER THE GREAT flood, the family of Noah and those who came after him grew in number until, as the years went on, the earth began to be full of people once more.

At that time, all the people in the world spoke the same language. They all lived happily together in a place called Shinar. But one day, these people found out they could make bricks out of their soil. All they had to do was mix water with the soil and then bake it till it was hard.

Then someone said:

"Let us build a great tower!" they cried. "A tower that reaches clear to Heaven!"

"Yes! Yes!" they all shouted. "Let us build a tower to Heaven, and then we shall be as mighty as God!"

And so the tower was begun. Many men helped to build it, and as the bricks began to pile up, the tower grew taller and taller. Finally it was so tall that the people on the ground looked like ants to the men working at the top of the tower.

"Look! Look!" cried the people. "The tower is taller than the tallest tree! We are greater than God, for we have built something much taller than anything God has ever made!"

Then a very strange thing happened!

"I am going to climb to the top of the tower!" cried one of the men.

"What did you say?" asked another man.

"Why are you two men making those strange sounds?" cried a third man.

And a fourth man turned to his brother and said:

"What is wrong with those men? They sound like monkeys chattering!"

But his brother looked at him in a puzzled way and said:

"I cannot understand a word you are saying!"

God had sent a punishment! God had put a strange language in every man's mouth, so that nobody understood anybody else. The people became so confused, they ran about like frightened geese, making strange noises at each other. Of course they could not build the tower any higher, for how could people build anything together when they could not speak the same language and couldn't understand one another?

The great Tower of Babel was never finished, and the people were scattered over the earth, each family settling in a different place and speaking a different language. That is how the different nations started, each with its own language.

COMPLETE THE SENTENCE.

1. Long ago all the people in the world spoke the
Same language.

2. The people wanted to build a _tower_ with its top in the sky.

3. God punished the people by mixing up their _language_.

4. God scattered the people all over the _world_.

5. The tower was called _Babel_.

~~Babel, world, tower, language, same language~~

MATCH THE COLUMNS.

A	B
1. In those days everyone spoke	tower
2. The people lived in	one language
3. They wanted to build a	mixing up their language
4. They built a tower of	Shinar
5. God punished them by	bricks

WHY did God stop the building of the Tower?
BECAUSE God was angry at the builders. First, the builders thought they could reach heaven and become like God.

Secondly, the goals of the builders became more important than human life. The builders worked day and night, and if a brick was lost or broken, there was great sorrow.

If a brick fell and killed someone, they became angry about the time lost. They were more concerned about the brick than about the life that was lost.

LANGUAGE CAN BE BEAUTIFUL

God was unhappy with the builders of the tower. So God decided to punish them in a very peculiar way.

God placed a strange language in each person's mouth. Nobody could understand what the other person was saying. Of course, they couldn't continue to build their foolish tower.

You see, language can help build as well as destroy. Language can be beautiful, as in poems and songs and books.

Language can also be ugly, as when we scream, or curse and use dirty words, or tell lies.

Language can make you a kid that everyone likes or a nerd that no one wants to talk to.

I am sure you are always meeting new kids and grown-ups too. What do you say when you meet new people for the first time? Remember, your first impression is very important. Usually, the first impression is how they judge you for a long time to come.

What will you say to these people when you meet them for the first time?

1. A new teacher in the synagogue school

   Hello. My name is Abigail.

2. A new rabbi in the synagogue

   Shalom.

3. A new classmate

   Hi. My name is Abbie. What's yours

4. A new friend of your parents

Abraham and Lot

ABRAHAM AND HIS nephew, Lot, were traveling through the desert, looking for a new home. They had brought their tents and all their cattle and sheep with them. They traveled for many days, until they came to the Land of Canaan.

"There is plenty of grass here for the cattle and sheep," said Abraham. "This shall be our new home."

And so Abraham and Lot set up their tents in the Land of Canaan. Their servants let the cattle and sheep into the green pastures.

All went well for a time, but one day, one of Lot's shepherds came to him and said:

"It is not fair! Your uncle's sheep are eating all the grass and drinking all the water! There is not enough room for all these sheep!"

Shortly after this, one of Abraham's shepherds came to him and said:

"Your nephew's sheep eat all the grass, while yours grow thin! They will die of thirst, for there is not enough water for all the sheep!"

Abraham and Lot tried to tell the shepherds there was plenty for all. But Lot's shepherds began to quarrel with Abraham's shepherds and Abraham was very troubled. He was a man of peace and hated quarrels. So he said to his nephew, Lot: "We are family, let there be no quarrel between you and me nor between your men and my men, for you and I are like brothers to each other. The whole land is before us; let us part. You shall have the first choice. If you will take the land on the right hand, then I will take the land on the left; or if you choose the land on the left, then I will take the right."

This was noble and generous of Abraham, for he was the older and could have claimed the first choice.

Lot looked over the green valley. The River Jordan wound in and out among the trees like a bright silver ribbon.

"My cattle and sheep will have lots of grass and water in this valley," thought Lot.

"I choose the valley," he said.

Abraham said:

"Yes, the land is beautiful, and there is no richer soil to be found anywhere! But remember, too, that the two cities of Sodom and Gomorrah are also on the plain of Jordan. The people in these cities are very wicked. They worship idols. Do you think you can be happy living among these wicked people?"

But Lot shrugged his shoulders and said:

"What other people do is none of my business. All I care about is the land. My sheep need plenty of grass and I need rich soil for my gardens. I have chosen this land and there I will stay!"

And so Lot took his wife and children and moved away to the new land he had chosen.

Abraham stayed in the land of Canaan and everyone loved him, for he was a very kind and peaceful man. God loved Abraham, too. After Lot had left to go to his new home, God said to Abraham:

"Lift up your eyes from this place and look east and west and north and south. All the land that you can see, mountains and valleys and plains, I will give to you and to your children and their children and those who come after them."

COMPLETE THE SENTENCE.

1. The shepherds of _Abraham_ and the shepherds of _Lot_ fought over the land.

2. Lot settled in the valley near _Sodom_ and _Gomorrah_ .

3. Abraham stayed in the land of _Canaan_ .

4. Everyone loved Abraham because he was good and _Kind_ .

5. God promised Abraham lots of _land_ .

6. Abraham said to Lot, "You and I are like _brothers_ to each other."

kind, Sodom, land, brothers, Gomorrah, Lot, Abraham, Canaan

MATCH THE COLUMNS.

A	B
1. Garden of	Abel
2. Noah's	Abraham's nephew
3. Tower of	Eden
4. Shabbat	Babel
5. Lot	Ark
6. Cain and	Day of Rest

WHY did Abraham allow Lot to choose first the land on which to live?

BECAUSE Abraham was a man of peace. Rather than have arguments or fights between his men and Lot's men, he gave Lot the pick of the land.

In Hebrew the word for peace is Shalom. Abraham was a true man of Shalom.

Shalom is so precious to us that it is both a greeting and a goodbye.

Shalom is so precious that we pray for it a number of times each day.

IT'S YOUR DECISION

Making a decision means picking and choosing. Grown-ups as well as kids are always making decisions. The options from which you choose are called choices.

Abraham gave Lot the first choice. He said, "You shall have the first choice. If you will take the land on the right hand, then I will take the land on the left; or if you choose the land on the left, then I will take the right." Abraham gave Lot the first choice because he had made a decision that Shalom (peace) between them was more important than wealth.

Lot made his decision to live near the evil cities of Sodom and Gomorrah and said, "My cattle and sheep will have lots of grass and water in this valley." Lot made his decision and chose the valley because he wanted to be wealthy.

Some choices and decisions are easy to make.

Which candy to buy? What TV programs to watch? What sweater to wear? But sometimes choices and decisions are difficult to make.

What would your decision be in these cases?

Your friend shows you tomorrow's test. Your friend says, "I will let you look at it before the exam." What do you do? _Say, "no thank you because that is cheating."_

You want to see a special movie. A friend says, "Lie about your age and you will be able to buy a cheaper ticket." What do you do? _Say, "no thank you because I don't lie."_

Abraham and The Three Angels

ABRAHAM AND HIS wife, Sarah, were very lonely, because they had no children. Every day they asked God to send them a child.

One day, as Abraham was sitting in the doorway of his tent, he saw three men walking in the hot sun. Abraham went to meet them and said:

"You must stop and rest in the shade of this tree. I will bring you water to wash your feet. And I will bring you bread to eat and cool milk to drink."

Then Abraham went inside the tent and said to Sarah:

"There are three men outside. They are tired and hungry. Bake three cakes for them to eat."

When the cakes were baked, Abraham took them to the men. After the men had eaten and rested, they stood up before Abraham and a great light shone all around them.

"Behold!" cried one of the men. "We are angels of the Lord. Where is your wife, Sarah?"

"She is in the tent!" said Abraham.

"Go to her and tell her God will send her a son," said the angel.

Although it was hard to believe, because Abraham and Sarah were old, Abraham shouted with joy. For now he knew that these strangers were really three angels whom God had sent to him with this great news.

The three angels went away, and Abraham called Sarah and told her the glad news. When Sarah learned that, at last, after all these years, she was to have a son, the tears rolled down her face and she laughed to herself.

God kept the promise and when a beautiful little boy was born to Abraham and Sarah, they called him Isaac, which means "laughter."

NAME THE RELATIVE. MATCH THE COLUMNS.

1. Adam's wife   Lot
2. Noah's sons   Sarah
3. Cain's brother   Eve
4. Abraham's nephew   Shem, Ham, and Japeth
5. Eve's husband   Abel
6. Cain's mother   Adam
7. Abraham's wife   Eve

COMPLETE THE SENTENCE.

1. Abraham and his wife _Sarah_ had no children.
2. Abraham called his son _Isaac_.
3. The word Isaac means _laughter_.
4. Abraham saw _three_ men walking in the _sun_.
5. "They are tired, bake three _cakes_ for them to eat."
6. A great _light_ shown around the men.
7. "Go tell her that _God_ will send her a son," said the _angel_.

God, light, Sarah, three, sun, Isaac, cakes, laughter, angel

WHY did Abraham welcome the three strangers?
BECAUSE Abraham was a good friend and neighbor to all people.

He liked people and people liked him. He and Sarah always welcomed travelers who passed by the large tent which was their home. If the travelers were hungry, food was given them. If they needed a bed to sleep in, they were put up for the night.

Abraham and Sarah were known for their kindness. When their guests thanked them for their hospitality, they would answer by saying that God was to be thanked, for it was the Lord who provides for all.

HACHNASAT ORCHIM

Wherever Abraham and Sarah lived, their home was always open to people in need.

The Rabbis say that Abraham's tent had four doors, one facing north, one east, one west, and one south. So a traveler coming from any direction would always find the door to Abraham's tent, where he could rest, eat, and drink.

The mitzvah of welcoming guests is called Hachnasat Orchim. There are many ways of performing the mitzvah of Hachnasat Orchim.

Suppose a new kid moved into your neighborhood.

How would you perform the mitzvah of Hachnasat Orchim?

I would invite the kid and his/her parents over to show them around in the naborhood.

How could your parents perform the mitzvah of Hachnasat Orchim if a new neighbor moved in?

They can bake cookies and bring them over to the new nabors house.

If the newcomers were Jewish, how would the rabbi perform the mitzvah of Hachnasat Orchim?

The rabbi would give him a saromony.

31

Abraham and Isaac

ISAAC GREW STRONG and tall and Abraham loved him very much. But sometimes God tests our faith and love to see how strong and true we are. The test God gave to Abraham was a very hard one. But even though it nearly broke Abraham's heart to do what God had asked of him, he obeyed. And no wonder Abraham was heartbroken! For this is what God had said to him:

"Abraham, take your son Isaac and go into the land of Moriah and when you come to the mountain about which I shall tell you, make of your son Isaac an offering to Me!"

Abraham could scarcely believe his ears. Why had God asked him to make such a sacrifice! Abraham's heart was heavy, and for one whole night, he paced back and forth in his tent, wringing his hands and crying. But when morning came, he was calm. His great wisdom and faith told him that God must have a good reason for asking him to do this thing.

Abraham said to Isaac:

"Come, my son, we are going up to the mountain."

Isaac was very happy. He skipped along the road beside his father, singing a merry song. When they reached the mountain, Abraham said:

"You must help me build an altar. We are going to give God a present."

When the altar was finished Isaac said, "What are we going to give to God, father?"

Abraham picked Isaac up in his arms and carried him to the altar.

"You are the gift, my son," he said.

But just then, God's voice came out of the sky.

"Abraham!" cried God. "You have proved that you would do whatever I asked. I shall give your son back to you. Look for another gift for me instead."

"Look, father!" cried Isaac. "There is a ram in the bushes!"

Through the happy tears in his eyes, Abraham saw a ram, caught by his horns in the bushes. He took the ram and made an offering of it to God.

God blessed Abraham for his great faith and sent him every good thing in life.

CHOOSE THE CORRECT ANSWER.

1. Isaac grew strong and tall, and _____ loved him very much.

2. God said to Abraham, "Take your son _____ to the land

of _____ and make of your son a _____ to me."

3. Abraham and Isaac went to Mount Moriah. Then Abraham placed

Isaac on the _____.

4. Just then God said, "You have proved yourself, look for another _____."

5. Through the happy tears in his eyes, Abraham saw a

_____.

6. Abraham took the ram and offered it to _____.

God, ram, Abraham, Isaac, gift, altar, offering, Moriah

MATCH THE COLUMNS.

1. I agreed to sacrifice my son Isaac because I trusted God.　　Abel

2. I was Abraham's son.　　Isaac

3. I was the first man in the world.　　Noah

4. I was the first woman in the world.　　Adam

5. My brother Cain killed me.　　Eve

6. I built an ark.　　Abraham

WHY did Isaac go willingly to be sacrificed?
BECAUSE Isaac honored his father by obeying and doing exactly as he was told.

The fifth commandment says, "Honor your father and your mother." Parents are very special people. They work very hard to raise you and to take care of you.

Your family is a team. You are an important member of that team. When all the members of the family do their part, then you have a winning team.

You can help by listening and obeying the captain of your team, your parents.

YOUR FAMILY

People in a family belong to each other. They share and take care of each other. Helping and sharing are important in Judaism. They are part of the holy way.

The ancient Rabbis had many quotations about the importance of the family.

Decipher this rabbinic quotation:

A	א
B	ב
C	ה
D	ד
E	,
F	ש
G	ג
H	ח
I	ת
J	כ
K	פ
L	ל
M	מ
N	ג
O	ר
P	פ
Q	ק
R	ר
S	ס
T	ט
U	ס
V	ר
W	ף
X	ז
Y	,
Z	ץ

שׁ ילעפ א יכעל סע ץלעמאשׁ א

יחט דנא ינך יודמיר.ס ינךטס

.סללאשׁ ילעפ ילדחף

What do you think the quotation means? _____

_____

Decipher this rabbinic quotation:

שׁלי סרסדץ טעדירהסעד סדץ שׁ

ילדחף רסדץ טעדירהסעד סך

ץלעמאשׁ.

What do you think the quotation means? _____

_____

Isaac and Rebecca

ONE DAY, ABRAHAM said to Eliezer, his servant:

"I am a very old man. Before I die, you must go and find a wife for my son, Isaac. Choose her from our people, and bring her back to this country."

You see, Abraham did not want Isaac to marry a woman of the people in the land where he was living, for they were all worshipers of idols, and would not teach their children the ways of the Lord.

The next day, Eliezer started on his journey, with the camels, and gifts of gold and silver. After a few days, he came to a city. Outside the city gates there was a well. Beside the well several young girls were filling jars with water.

"May I have a drink of water?" Eliezer asked one of the girls. But she would not answer him. Then another girl, with lovely black hair and kind brown eyes, smiled at Eliezer and said:

"Drink, sir," she said; and she quickly lowered the pitcher from her shoulder and gave him water to drink. When he had finished drinking she said:

"Let me draw water for your camels also, until they have enough."

"You are very kind," said Eliezer. "What is your name?"

"I am Rebecca, daughter of Bethuel," answered the girl.

Then Eliezer knew that God had led him to this place, for Abraham was this girl's uncle. Eliezer bowed before Rebecca and said: "Take these jewels as a gift".
"I cannot take these jewels," said Rebecca, "but I will go and ask my father if you can rest at our house".

When Rebecca reached home, she told her brother Laban about the man at the well. Laban went to bring Eliezer home. Then Eliezer said:

"I am the servant of Abraham," he said, "and I have been sent to your land by my master to seek a wife for his son, Isaac. My master told me that God would give me a sign so that I would know the right woman. And I asked God to let the right one offer water to my camels as well as to me. It was your daughter who was kind enough to do this. In the name of my master, Abraham, I ask the hand of your daughter in marriage to my master's son, Isaac."

Rebecca's father said:

"Yes, I believe that Abraham is a wise and good man. His name is well-known throughout this land. I shall tell my daughter to prepare herself for the journey."

But the girl's mother was not quite so anxious for her beloved daughter to leave home, perhaps never to return.

"Please," she begged her husband, "let Rebecca speak for herself."

Rebecca came into the room, and her father told her what Abraham's servant had said. She stood with her eyes lowered.

"Well, my daughter," asked her father, "are you willing to go?"

Rebecca looked at her mother, whose eyes were filled with tears. Then she said softly, "Yes, father, I will go."

And so Eliezer and Rebecca started on their journey back to Abraham's country. When they had traveled a few days, they saw a man coming towards them through the fields.

Then Eliezer said to Isaac, "This is Rebecca. I have brought her to be your wife."

When Isaac and Rebecca looked at each other, they both knew right away that it was indeed God's will for them to be together as long as they both should live.

WHO AM I? MATCH THE COLUMNS.

A	B
1. I am Abraham's servant.	Sarah
2. I am Isaac's mother.	Eliezer
3. I married Isaac.	Laban
4. I am Abraham's nephew.	Eve
5. I built an Ark.	Adam
6. I am the first man.	Noah
7. I am the first woman.	Rebecca
8. I am the brother of Rebecca.	Lot

CHOOSE THE CORRECT ANSWER.

1. Abraham did not want Isaac to marry an

idol worshipper.

2. _Eliezer_ was Abraham's trusted servant.

3. _Rebecca_ was the daughter of Bethuel.

4. _Laban_ was Rebecca's brother.

5. Rebecca drew water for Eliezer and his

camels.

camels, Laban, idol, Eliezer, Rebecca

WHY did Rebecca, who was very rich, go to the well to draw water?
BECAUSE, the Rabbis said, by going to the well, she could meet people and help them.

Helping people in time of need is called Gemilat Chasadim.

Rebecca went out of her way to do the mitzvah of Gemilat Chasadim.

THE GEMILAT CHASADIM MAZE

Rebecca was a young lady who went out of her way to help people.

Helping people and animals is called Gemilat Chasadim.

Let's see if you can perform the mitzvah of Gemilat Chasadim.

Begin at Start and follow the maze. Discuss each situation.

How could you help in each case?

How could you perform the mitzvah of Gemilat Chasadim?

If someone could not care for there pet for the day, I would take care of their pet and they would not have to pay.

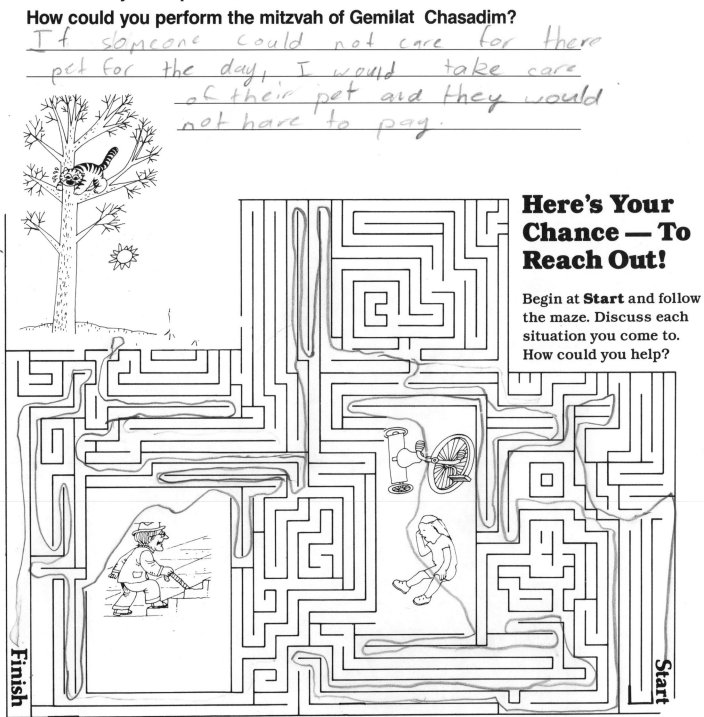

Here's Your Chance — To Reach Out!

Begin at **Start** and follow the maze. Discuss each situation you come to. How could you help?

Jacob and Esau

ISAAC AND REBECCA had two twin sons, Jacob and Esau. Esau was just a few minutes older than his brother Jacob, and although these two brothers were twins, they were not at all alike. Esau was very hairy. His hands and neck and arms were covered with thick, red hair, but Jacob's hands and neck were smooth. Esau grew up to be a strong man and he loved to hunt in the woods and mountains for deer.

But Jacob was quiet and thoughtful, staying at home and caring for the flocks of his father.

Now in those long ago days, when the father of a family died, the oldest son received twice as much of his father's flocks and land as the younger sons. This was called the oldest sons birthright. The oldest son became the leader of the family and received his father's blessings.

One day, Esau came home after hunting all day in the fields. Jacob was cooking a mess of pottage. Esau had not eaten all day and he was very hungry. The food smelled so good that he cried out:

"I would sell my birthright for that mess of pottage!"

"But surely you must be joking," said Jacob.

"What do I care about a lot of sheep and land I will not have until my father dies," said Esau. "All I care about now is food! Give me the pottage and the birthright is yours!"

"Do you promise?" asked Jacob.

Jacob set the food before his brother. As he watched Esau gobble up the pottage, Jacob thought that Esau was very foolish. He was so greedy for a dish of food that he had sold his precious birthright for a mess of pottage!

CHOOSE THE CORRECT ANSWER.

1. Jacob and Esau were

_____.

   a. twins

   b. the sons of Abraham

   c. very much alike

2. Esau was _____.

   a. a farmer

   b. a hunter

   c. a scholar

3. Jacob was a _____.

   a. hunter

   b. farmer

   c. quiet man who cared for his

      sheep

4. Esau sold the birthright to Jacob

for _____.

   a. a large sum of money

   b. a mess of pottage

   c. five sheep

WHY did Jacob deserve the birthright?
BECAUSE, the Rabbis say, Esau was wicked from
the day that he was born.

Both Jacob and Esau tried to influence those around
them.

Jacob tried to turn them toward God and mitzvot.
Esau tried to turn them to evil and away from God.

THEY HELPED MAKE A BETTER WORLD

There are lots of people who want to influence you. Most of them, like Jacob, try to influence you to become a better person. Your family, your teachers, your rabbi, and your friends help you to learn new things and become a better person.

Here are two American Jews whose influence and deeds helped make the world a better and happier place.

NATHAN STRAUSS 1848–1931

Nathan Strauss was born in Germany and came to America when he was six. As a young man he worked in his father's glassware business. When he was twenty-six, he and his brother became partners in R.H. Macy and Company. Two years later they bought the entire department store.

Nathan Strauss wanted to do something worthwhile with his riches. He gave money to many charities and projects. His greatest concern was for the health and welfare of poor babies.

He set up laboratories to test and treat milk. Then he started the Strauss Milk Fund, which distributed pasteurized milk to the poor.

In 1892 there was widespread unemployment. That winter many poor people couldn't afford to buy coal to heat their homes. Nathan Strauss made life easier for those who were in need. He arranged for baskets of coal to be sold for five cents each.

He served meals for one cent in his milk stations.

Nathan Strauss gave about two-thirds of all his money to projects in the land of Israel. The Israelis wanted to show how grateful they were. When he was eighty, Natanya, a colony near Tel Aviv, was established in his honor.

Nathan Strauss was called "The Great Giver." He worked hard, made a fortune, and then spent his life helping others.

LOUIS BRANDEIS 1856–1941

Louis Brandeis decided to become a lawyer when he was fifteen years old. He chose this career because he wanted to help people by making sure they were treated justly and equally.

Brandeis was the youngest student ever to attend Harvard Law School, and probably the best. He was most interested in public interest law. He refused to accept payment because he wanted to remain independent and not be influenced by money.

In July 1910, Brandeis was called upon to settle a strike in the clothing industry. The workers were Jewish, and so were the bosses. Brandeis got the employers to see the workers' needs. He made the workers understand the owners' problems. In September 1910, both sides agreed to a settlement and signed the "Protocol of Peace."

Louis Brandeis loved the Jewish people and was a devoted Zionist. In 1916, he became the first Jew to serve on the Supreme Court of the United States.

Louis D. Brandeis saw that the "little people" of the world needed a big voice to be raised for their protection. He raised his for them.

Jacob Receives His Brother's Blessing

ISAAC, THE FATHER of Jacob and Esau, was now an old man. He could no longer see, for his eyes had become blind. One day, he said to his older son, Esau:

"Go into the woods and bring back a deer. Cook the meat and bring it to me. Then I will give you my blessing."

But when Isaac's wife, Rebecca, heard these words, she said to Jacob:

"You should receive the blessing instead of your brother. The birthright is yours."

Then Rebecca told Jacob to bring two young goats from the flocks in the fields.

"I will cook a dish of meat," she said, "and you can take it to your father. But you must cover your body with these goatskins. Your brother is very hairy. When your father feels the goatskin, he will think you are Esau and give you his blessing."

Jacob took the meat to his father and said:

"I have come for my blessing, father."

"You speak with the voice of Jacob," said Isaac. "Come closer and let me touch you."

Jacob held out his arm.

"You must be Esau," said Isaac, "for you are covered with hair."

Then he placed his hand on Jacob's head and said:

"I bless you above all others, to be leader of your brothers. May God go with you all thy days and guide you in holy ways."

Soon after this, Esau came to his father's bedside.

"Here is your meat, father," he said. "Please give me your blessing."

Then Isaac knew what he had done.

"It is too late, my son," he said. "I have given your blessing to Jacob."

Esau angrily cried:

"When my father dies, I shall kill my brother!"

Rebecca was afraid. She said to Jacob:

"You must go to my brother Laban's house and stay until I send for you."

And so Jacob had to leave his home and travel to a far country.

It was better that Jacob's descendants, those who came after him, should have the blessing, than that Esau's people should have had it; for Jacob's people worshiped God, and Esau's people walked in the way of the idols, and became wicked.

CHOOSE THE CORRECT ANSWER.

1. Rebecca said, "You should receive the blessing instead of your brother _____."

   a. Abraham

   b. Esau

   c. Noah

2. "You must be Esau," said Isaac, "for you are covered with _____."

   a. skin

   b. a blanket

   c. hair

3. "When my father dies, I shall kill my _____."

   a. sister

   b. mother

   c. brother

4. Jacob's people worshipped _____, and Esau's people walked in the way of idols.

   a. cats

   b. God

   c. money

MATCH THE COLUMNS.

1. Birthright

2. Pottage

3. Esau

4. Jacob

5. Rebecca

6. Eliezer

7. Isaac

8. Eliezer's camels

Given water by Rebecca

Servant of Abraham

Mother of Jacob and Esau

Favorite son of his mother

Special blessing

Hunter

Selling price of the birthright

Rebecca's husband

WHY did Rebecca want Jacob to get the blessing? **BECAUSE** Rebecca saw that Esau would be a poor leader to carry out God's plan for the Jewish people.

A leader should be a caring person with intelligence, who wants to make the world a better and happier place.

Rebecca knew that a person who likes to kill and who would give up the blessing for a bowl of pottage would be a poor leader.

YOUR FIVE SENSES

God created a beautiful world filled with wondrous creations. God gave us rainbows to see, flowers to smell, fruits to taste, music to hear, and animals to pet and play with.

We enjoy God's world because of our five senses: sight, hearing, smell, taste, and touch.

Isaac, who was blind, used the sense of touch and hearing to identify his sons.

What can you learn through your five senses.
With your eyes (SEEING)

You can read,

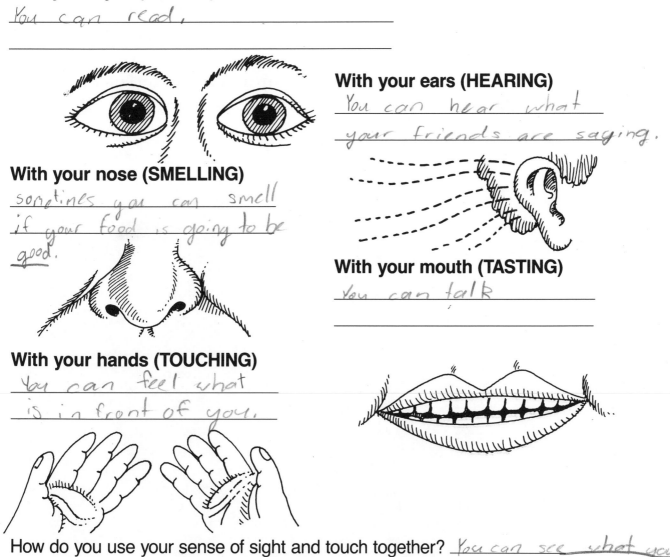

With your ears (HEARING)

You can hear what your friends are saying.

With your nose (SMELLING)

sometimes you can smell if your food is going to be good.

With your mouth (TASTING)

You can talk

With your hands (TOUCHING)

You can feel what is in front of you.

How do you use your sense of sight and touch together? *You can see what you*

How do you use your sense of taste and smell together? *Tast what you smell*

How does the Havdalah ceremony use all five senses? *read, touch, talk, hear, smell (feel)(mouth)(ear) and see what you read.*

47

Jacob's Ladder

JACOB, THE SON of Isaac and Rebecca, was on his way to visit his uncle, who lived far away in another country.

Jacob walked all day long, and when night time came, he was very tired. He wished he were home, so he could sleep in his own bed. He felt very lonely. There was no place to lie down except the hard ground. Jacob's only pillow was a stone. But soon he was fast asleep.

The bright stars twinkled kindly down upon him. The night was very still. Jacob dreamed that he heard music. But where could the music be coming from so late at night?

All around him shone a bright light. In the light, Jacob saw a great shining ladder that reached clear to heaven. Beautiful angels were going up and down the ladder, singing the most wonderful song Jacob had ever heard.

Then Jacob heard the voice of God.

"Do not be afraid," said God. "You are not alone. I shall be with you always." Then the ladder and the angels were gone.

Jacob awoke and looked up at the bright stars.

"I guess it was just a dream," he thought.

But he did not feel lonely any more. He went back to sleep, and when he awoke, the sun was shining. Jacob remembered his dream. He knew that he would never be afraid again, because God had promised to be with him always.

"Oh, God," he cried aloud. "If you will bless me on my journey and bring me back to my father's house in peace, I shall offer you one-tenth of all with which you blessed me."

Then Jacob took the stone which he had used for a pillow and set it in the ground, and poured oil over it and made it an altar to God. Jacob called the place Beth-el which means the House of God.

Excellent

MATCH THE COLUMNS.

1. Dreamed of a ladder   Isaac
2. Sold his birthright   Jacob
3. Covered his arms with goatskins   Jacob
4. Promised God one-tenth of his blessings   House of God
5. Beth El   Jacob
6. Was a hunter   Esau
7. The father of Jacob and Esau   Esau

COMPLETE THE SENTENCES.

1. Jacob dreamed he saw a ___ladder___ that reached into heaven.
2. Jacob was on his way to visit his ___uncle___ who lived far away.
3. Jacob heard the voice of ___God___ say, "You are not alone. I shall be with you always."
4. Jacob took the stone which he had used for a ___pillow___ and made it an ___altar___ to God.
5. "I offer you ___one-tenth___ of all with which you bless me."
6. Jacob was the son of Isaac and ___Rebecca___.

~~God, pillow, altar, ladder, uncle, Rebecca, one-tenth~~

WHY did Jacob decide to give one-tenth of his earnings to charity?

BECAUSE this was Jacob's way of saying thank you for all the good things God had given him.

In ancient Israel, the Jews were required to give **mah-asur** (one-tenth of their crops) to charity.

Today, there are many Jews all over the world who contribute a tithe (**mah-asur**) of their earnings to charity.

When you give a "tithe," you are thanking God for watching over you and giving you a share of God's wealth.

WHOM WILL YOU SUPPORT?

When you give a "tithe," you are thanking God for watching over you and giving you a share of God's wealth.

Suppose that when you become an adult, you decide to *mah-asur* your earnings. How would you distribute your money?

Look at this community map. Decide which three places will receive your support. Tell why you would contribute to those institutions.

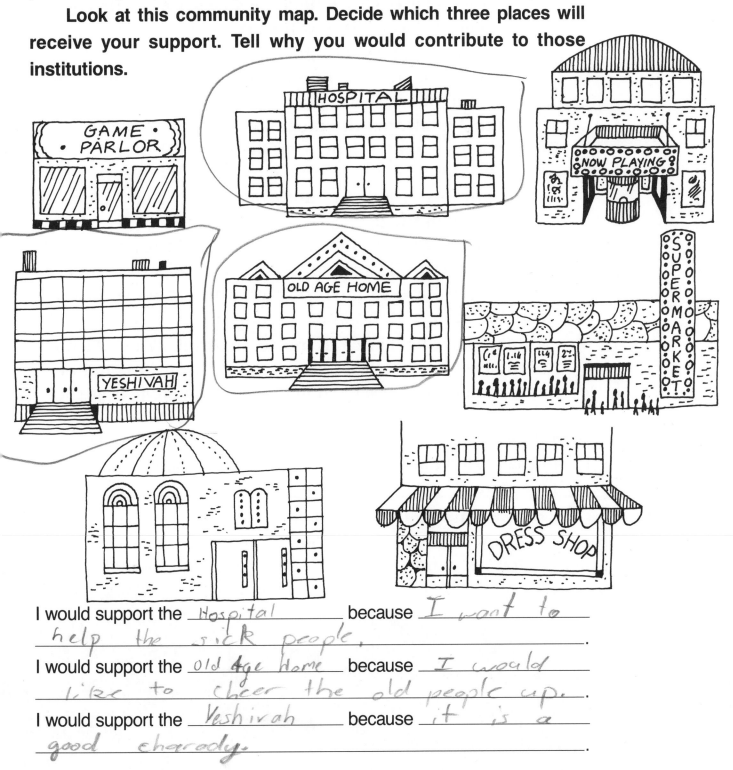

I would support the ___Hospital___ because ___I want to help the sick people___.

I would support the ___Old Age Home___ because ___I would like to cheer the old people up___.

I would support the ___Yeshivah___ because ___it is a good charady___.

Jacob Wins Rachel

AFTER JACOB'S DREAM about the ladder, he felt strong and ready to go on with his journey eastward, to the land where his uncle Laban lived.

As he was crossing a field, he saw a well, with a great stone over it. Beside the well were some shepherds and their sheep. Jacob said to the men:

"Brothers, do you know a man called Laban, the grandson of Nahor?"

"Yes," answered the men, "we know him well. Look, here comes Laban's daughter Rachel, with her father's sheep."

"But it is not time to water the sheep," said Jacob, "it is still early in the day."

"But the stone is so heavy," answered the shepherds, "that we must wait until all the flocks are gathered here. Then we all have to push on the stone to move it away from the mouth of the well."

Just then, Rachel came up to the well. When Jacob looked at her, he saw that she was very beautiful, and he loved her at once. He walked up to the great stone over the mouth of the well and with one mighty push, he sent it rolling to one side. Then the shepherds let their sheep drink, and Jacob led Rachel's sheep to the well and drew water for her sheep.

"Who are you?" she asked.

"I am your cousin, Jacob."

Rachel ran to tell her father that Jacob had come to visit him. Laban came to meet Jacob.

"You must come to live in my house like my own son," Laban said. "You can work for me and I will pay you well."

"I do not want wages," said Jacob. "I want Rachel for my wife."

"Very well," said Laban; "work for me for seven years. Then Rachel will be your wife."

For seven years, Jacob worked very hard. But the seven years seemed like seven days, for Rachel was always near. When the seven years had passed, Jacob said to Laban:

"It is time for Rachel to become my bride."

Now Laban had an older daughter named Leah. She was not as pretty as Rachel, and her father was afraid she might not find a husband. Laban decided to deceive Jacob. He ordered his servants to prepare a great wedding feast.

On the day of the feast, Jacob's bride wore a very heavy veil over her face. After she and Jacob were married, she lifted the veil.

"You are not Rachel!" cried Jacob. "You are Leah!"

Jacob was very angry. But Laban said:

"Work for me another seven years and Rachel will be your wife."

Jacob promised to work another seven years. After seven more years there was another wedding feast. But this time, it was Rachel who was the bride. Jacob was very happy.

CHOOSE THE CORRECT ANSWER.

1. "Do you know a man called

_____, the grandson

of Nahor?"

a. Abraham

(b) Laban

c. Noah

2. "I want _____ for my

wife."

a. Sarah

(b) Rachel

c. Eve

3. "You are not Rachel!" cried

Jacob. "You are

_____."

a. Sarah

(b) Leah

c. Judy

4. "Here comes Laban's daughter

Rachel, with her father's

_____."

a. airplane

(b) sheep

c. donkeys

WHO SAID OR DID IT.

A

1. I stole my brother's birthright.

2. I wrested with an angel.

3. I forgave my brother for cheating me.

4. I went to live with my uncle Laban.

5. I was a hunter.

6. I married my cousins Leah and Rachel.

WHICH BROTHER?

B

JACOB

ESAU

WHY did Laban trick Jacob and force him to stay for
another seven years?
BECAUSE, the Rabbis say, Jacob was an excellent farmer and a successful shepherd.

Under Jacob's skillful care, Laban's flocks and crops
kept increasing. Laban became a very wealthy man
because of Jacob's skills. So Laban wanted to become
even richer and kept Jacob for another seven years.

SPECIAL GIFTS

God created all of us with a brain and with special skills and gifts. People with special skills and gifts have made our world more beautiful, healthier, and happier.

Inventors with great ideas have designed wonderful machines like spaceships and automobiles and televisions.

Artists, writers, and musicians with special skills have made our world more beautiful and happier.

Doctors and scientists with special skills have made our world healthier and saved many lives.

Jacob was a successful shepherd and farmer with special skills.

Of course, you don't become an athlete, or a doctor, or a teacher by magic. It requires lots of hard work and study and hours of practice. God gave us special gifts so that we can continue to make the world better and happier.

Complete this inventory by listing your present skills, your future skill goals and the things you need to do to reach those goals.

Topic: SPORTS

Present Skills — I am able to _____

Future Goal — I want to be able to _____

To reach my goal I must _____

Topic: SCHOOL WORK

Present Skills — I am able to _____

Future Goal — I want to be able to _____

To reach my goal I must _____

Topic: BEHAVIOR

Present Skills — I am able to _____

Future Goal — I want to be able to _____

To reach my goal I must _____

Topic: RELIGIOUS SCHOOL

Present Skills — I am able to _____

Future Goal — I want to be able to _____

To reach my goal I must _____

Jacob's Name Is Changed

AFTER MANY YEARS, Jacob was going home. For he had heard the voice of God saying:

"Take your family and your servants and all your flocks and go back to the land of Canaan."

Jacob set out on his journey with all his family. Behind them came the servants, with hundreds of sheep, goats, donkeys, and camels.

After several days, the travelers came near the land where Esau, Jacob's brother, lived. Jacob sent some of his servants ahead to see Esau.

"Tell my brother I hope he is no longer angry with me," Jacob said.

But the servants soon came back and said:

"Your brother is coming to meet you with four hundred men!"

Then Jacob divided his people into two camps.

"If Esau attacks one camp, the other will be safe," he thought.

Then he took his finest sheep and goats and said to his servants:

"Take these to my brother as my gift. Tell him I am coming to meet him."

That night, Jacob could not sleep. He walked up and down in the moonlight, outside his camp. Suddenly, he heard a noise behind him. Before he could turn around, a strong arm went around his shoulders. He was thrown to the ground. Then Jacob saw a man standing over him. The man was very tall and strong.

"Who are you?" Jacob cried. But the man did not answer.

All night long, Jacob fought with this mighty man. Early in the morning, Jacob threw the man to the ground.

And the man said: "Let me go, for the day is breaking."

And Jacob said: "I will not let you go until you bless me." And the man said:

"What is your name?"

And Jacob answered, "Jacob is my name."

Then the man said:

Then the angel said:

"Your name shall no more be called Jacob, but Israel, that is, 'He who wrestles with God.' For you have wrestled with God and with men, and you have won."

And the angel blessed him there.

WHO SAID IT? CHOOSE THE CORRECT PERSON.

1. "Take your family and your servants and all your flocks and go back to the land of Canaan." _____

2. "Tell my brother I hope he is no longer angry with me."

_____

3. "Let me go, for the day is breaking." _____

4. "I will not let you go until you bless me." _____

5. "Your name shall no more be called Jacob, but Israel." _____

angel, God, Jacob, angel, Jacob

CHOOSE THE CORRECT ANSWER.

1. "Take your _____ and your servants and all your flocks and go back to the land of _____."

2. "Tell my _____ I hope he is no longer angry with me," said Jacob.

3. "Your brother is coming to meet you with _____ men."

4. And Jacob said, "I will not let you go till you _____ me."

5. "Your name shall no more be called _____ but _____."

6. "If _____ attacks one _____, the other will be safe."

Israel, bless, four hundred, Esau, family, Canaan, brother, Jacob, camp

WHY did God change Jacob's name to Israel?
BECAUSE, the Torah tells us, "he wrestled with God and won."

The name Israel, in Hebrew *Yisrael,* is made up of two Hebrew words: *Yisra,* which means "to wrestle," and *El,* which means "God."

Jacob's new name was also a new start in his life. Jacob was no more the cowardly boy who ran away from Esau. Now he was a grown man, strong, fearless, very rich, and the father of a very large family.

Now the new man Israel, the man who had won a wrestling match with God, could face his angry brother

without fear.

WHAT'S IN A NAME?

In ancient times, names were given in connection with events in the family, the community, or the world.

The name Esau comes from the Hebrew word *ah-seh* ("to make"). Esau was born with as much hair as a "fully-made" mature man.

Jacob was given the Hebrew name Yaakov because he held on to the *ay-kev* ("heel") of Esau.

Today, among Jews, it is customary to name a child after a beloved dead relative.

1. Do you know how your Hebrew name was chosen? _____

_____

MIRRY

JOSEPH

ADAM

יְהוּדָה

גֵּרְשׁוֹן

 רְאוּבֵן

2. Were you named for a relative? _____

_____

3. Ask your family to recall the ideas or feelings involved in choosing your Hebrew name. _____

_____

ABBY

אֶפְרַיִם

4. Have you had any nicknames? _____

_____

SARA

דָּן

5. How did you get those names? _____

_____

6. What do these nicknames say about you?

_____

AARON

NOAH

JUDAH

Finding unusual names for a group or a club has become a popular indoor sport. Pretend that your temple is forming a new youth club and they are looking for a name, in Hebrew or in English, to express its identity. Choose a name for your club.

Esau Forgives Jacob

JACOB WAS ENCAMPED with his household near his old homeland. He was no longer the poor young man who had left this land so many years ago. Now he was rich and had many flocks of fine sheep, cattle, and goats.

Jacob sent some of his servants ahead to see his brother Esau. When they returned, they said:

"Your brother is coming to meet you with four hundred men!"

"Then he must still be angry with me," said Jacob, "and is coming to attack us. We will divide ourselves into two camps."

Then Jacob took some of his finest sheep and goats and said to his servants:

"Take these as my gifts to my brother. Tell him I wish to find favor in his sight."

The next day, as Jacob stood in the doorway of his tent, he saw a great cloud of dust in the distance. Then he heard the sound of galloping horses.

"It is my brother Esau, and his men!" cried Jacob.

He called Leah and Rachel and all his children together.

Into the camp rode the four hundred. Ahead of them rode a tall man with flashing black eyes.

"Halt!" cried the man. He jumped from his horse and stood before Jacob. Jacob bowed down to him seven times. Then Esau threw his arms around Jacob and kissed him. Jacob's heart was filled with joy.

·When Esau looked around at Jacob's sons and daughters, he said:

"Who are all these people?"

"They are the children God has given me," said Jacob.

"You should not have sent me all those fine animals," said Esau, "for I have enough of my own."

"I want you to keep them, with my blessing," said Jacob. "For I see you are pleased with me."

"Very well," said Esau. "Now let us travel on."

The brothers then traveled their separate ways. Esau went back to his home and Jacob went to the Land of Canaan. He built an altar and thanked God for leading him safely back to his homeland.

CHOOSE THE CORRECT ANSWER.

1. "Your brother is coming to meet

you with _____."

    a. four hundred men

    b. three hundred goats

    c. five hundred gerbils

2. Jacob said, "Take these as gifts

to my _____."

    a. mother

    b. brother

    c. doctor

3. He called Leah and

_____ and all his

children together.

    a. Sarah

    b. Rachel

    c. Sabrina

4. "I want you to keep them, with

my _____," said Jacob.

    a. horse

    b. blessing

    c. television

WHO DID IT? CHOOSE THE CORRECT ANSWER.

1. Changed Jacob's name? _____

2. Married Rachel? _____

3. Moved the stone from the well? _____

4. Worked for Laban? _____

5. Played a trick on Jacob? _____

6. Dreamed he saw a ladder? _____

7. Threatened to kill Jacob? _____

Esau, Laban, Jacob, Jacob, angel, Jacob, Jacob

WHY did Jacob send a gift of sheep and goats to his brother Esau?

BECAUSE Jacob's goal was to make peace with his brother Esau.

Who should make the first move? Who should give in first? It takes a very big person to apologize.

Sometimes a gift, sometimes a simple phrase such as "I'm sorry" or "Let's be friends," can help reach the friendship goal.

When Esau saw the gifts of his brother Jacob and the peaceful men and women in his family, his hate turned into brotherly love.

WHAT'S YOUR GOAL?

Jacob's goal was to make peace with his brother Esau. Goals are not always easy to reach. Just watch a football, basketball, or hockey game and you can see that it requires lots of effort to score a goal.

Scoring a football, volleyball, or hockey goal requires a team effort and cooperation by all team members.

Individual goals also require lots of hard work.

If your goal is to become a good student, then you will have to study hard to achieve that goal.

If your goal is to become a good athlete, then you will have to practice to achieve that goal.

If your goal is to become a good musician, then you will have to work long and hard to achieve that goal.

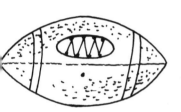
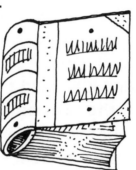

WRITE A PERSONAL GOAL FOR TODAY

_____

List the things you will have to do to reach the goal.

_____

_____

Write a goal for tomorrow. _____

_____

_____

Think back over yesterday. Write a goal you achieved that needed the cooperation of others. _____

_____

_____

Joseph's Coat of Many Colors

JACOB HAD TWELVE sons. He loved all his sons dearly, but he loved his son Joseph best of all. Joseph was a bright boy. He watched his father's sheep very well, so that no harm came to them.

Somehow, Joseph had the mark of a leader, and his father was very proud of him.

One day, Jacob called Joseph to his side.

"My son, I have a gift for you," he said. "It is a coat that was made just for you."

"Oh, father," cried Joseph, "I have never seen such a wonderful coat! It has so many colors in it! It is like a rainbow woven into cloth. Surely it must belong to a king, it is so rich and elegant!"

Jacob smiled and held the coat for Joseph to try.

Joseph put the coat on. It fit him just right.

"I like the coat very much, father," he said. "It is nice and warm. It makes me feel safe."

Joseph ran to find his brothers. He could hardly wait to show his wonderful coat of many colors. But when his brothers saw the coat, they were very jealous.

"Look at Joseph!" said one of the brothers. "He looks just like a parrot!"

"No!" cried another brother. "He looks like a walking rainbow!"

Jacob felt sad because his sons had treated Joseph so badly.

"My sons have forgotten what I have taught them," he said, "that God wants them to love each other and be kind to each other. Some day they will be sorry for the way they have treated Joseph!"

Joseph The Dreamer

ONE NIGHT, JOSEPH dreamed that he and his brothers were in the fields. They were binding sheaves of grain. Suddenly, the sheaves of Joseph's brothers stood in a circle around Joseph's sheaf and bowed down to it. When Joseph told his brothers about this dream, they cried:

"Does that mean you will rule over us some day? You, a shepherd boy?"

Then they laughed and whispered among themselves.

The next night, Joseph had another dream. This time, eleven stars came and bowed down before him. Then the moon and the sun bowed down to him.

"What a strange dream I had last night," he said to his brothers one morning. "I dreamed that the sun and the moon and eleven stars all bowed down to me as if I were a king!"

Now Joseph's father overheard him tell his brothers about this dream, and he knew the brothers were already so jealous they could hardly speak to Joseph. He knew this story about the second dream would anger them even more.

Joseph's brothers became very angry.

"I suppose you think the eleven stars were your eleven brothers," cried one.

"And the sun and moon were your father and mother," cried another brother. "Who are you, that your own father should bow down to you!"

Joseph's brothers hated him more than ever. They called him "the foolish dreamer."

You see, dreams are thought to be very important and people are always trying to figure out their meanings.

Jacob wondered about Joseph's two dreams, even though he pretended that he did not think they meant anything.

CHOOSE THE CORRECT ANSWER.

1. Jacob had _____ sons.

   a. twelve

   b. one hundred

   c. one thousand

2. _____ had the mark of a leader.

   a. Noah

   b. Joseph

   c. Eve

3. Jacob felt sad because his sons treated _____ badly.

   a. Joseph

   b. Abraham

   c. Esau

4. "I dreamed that the sun and the moon and eleven stars all bowed down to me as if I were a _____!"

   a. janitor

   b. king

   c. pussycat

5. Joseph's brothers _____ him more than ever.

   a. loved

   b. hated

   c. fed

MATCH THE COLUMNS.

A	B
1. Dreamed he was a king	Jacob
2. Were angry at Joseph	Jacob
3. Loved his son Joseph best of all	the brothers
4. Gave Joseph a beautiful coat	Joseph
5. Had twelve sons	Jacob

WHY were the brothers angry at Joseph?
BECAUSE Jacob played favorites and loved Joseph more than his other sons. The brothers were also angry at Joseph for acting superior. Joseph made the brothers angry by bragging about his dreams and parading around with his beautiful new coat.

THE BIG BRAGGER

It's not that Simmy is boring—she's more than okay. Simmy can play basketball, do card tricks, and best of all can sing like a bird.

The only problem with her is that she is always boasting how much money her family has.

"We have a great big Olympic swimming pool," crows Simmy. "And," boasts Simmy, "we go on vacation three times a year."

Matthew is having a birthday party next week and he has invited all the kids in the class.

Matthew doesn't want to invite boaster Simmy.

You see, Matthew's family live in a small apartment and they are not rich—in fact they are poor. Matthew's father is laid up in bed, and his mother works to support the family.

Matthew is afraid Simmy will make fun of him and his family.

"What do you think I ought to do?" asks Matthew.

Think of several things that Matthew can do. _____

_____

Now, choose the idea that is best. _____

Explain. _____

_____

MISTER LOUDMOUTH

Herky is a good athlete and he makes sure that everyone knows it.

"I'm the fastest runner in the whole school," boasts Herky. "And don't forget," he continues, "I can tumble better than anyone."

"I'm sick and tired of listening to that bigmouth," yells Iris.

"His bragging makes me sick," adds David.

"It isn't easy being his friend," complains Rebecca.

"As a matter of fact," adds George, "Mr. Loudmouth asked me to help him with his Hebrew homework. I don't know what to do."

Think of several different things George can do. _____

_____

Now, choose the idea that is best. _____

Explain. _____

_____

Joseph in Slavery

ONE DAY, JACOB said to his son Joseph:

"Your brothers are far away in the fields. Go and see if all is well with them."

Joseph put on his beautiful coat of many colors and set off to find his brothers.

At last Joseph found them but they were not happy to see him.

"Here he comes," cried one brother. "Let us kill him."

But Joseph's brother Reuben was more kind hearted and he could not bear to see young Joseph killed.

"Wait!" he cried. "Do not kill him. Throw him into the pit, but let us not have our own brother's blood upon our hands!"

Just then Joseph came running up to them.

"Hello!" he cried. "Father sent me to ..."

But Joseph never finished what he had started to say. One brother threw him to the ground. Two others tied his hands and feet together. Then they threw him into a deep pit and left him there alone.

Late in the afternoon, one of the brothers saw a long line of men and camels moving across the desert.

"Look," he said, "it is a caravan of Midianites , on their way to Egypt! Let us get Joseph from the pit and sell him."

They drew him out of the pit, and they sold him as a slave to a band of Midianites who were on their way to Egypt with their caravan.

When Reuben came from the field where he had been watching sheep, he looked into the pit.

"Where is Joseph?" he cried.

"We sold him as a slave. He is on his way to Egypt," said the brothers.

Then the brothers killed a goat, and put its blood on Joseph's coat.

When they reached home, they told their father that Joseph had been eaten by a wild beast.

They all pretended to be very sad.

"See, father," they cried out, "we have found this coat. But we have not found Joseph! We do not know if this is Joseph's coat or not. Can you tell?"

How could poor old Jacob mistake the wonderful coat he had given the son he loved so dearly? There was no other coat like it in all the land. The old man fell upon his knees and hugged the coat and cried over it.

His sons felt guilty when they saw how terribly grieved their father was. But it was too late now to bring Joseph back. Jacob mourned his son Joseph for many days, and soon the coat became spotted with the tears Jacob wept for the son he thought was dead.

CHOOSE THE CORRECT ANSWER.

1. "Your _____ are far away in the fields. Go see if all is well with them."

2. Joseph put on his beautiful _____.

3. "Do not kill him. Throw him into the _____."

4. "We sold him as a _____."

5. Jacob mourned his son _____ for many days.

6. They sold him as a slave to the _____ who were on their way to Egypt.

slave, Joseph, Midianites, brothers, pit, coat

MATCH THE COLUMNS.

A	B
1. Had a coat of many colors	Reuben
2. Gave Joseph a beautiful coat	Midianites
3. Sold Joseph as a slave	Joseph
4. Took Joseph to Egypt	Jacob
5. Did not want to kill Joseph	the brothers

WHY did the brothers decide to sell Joseph as a slave?
BECAUSE despite their jealousy the brothers still remembered that Joseph was their brother. Somehow, it seemed that selling him as a slave was better than killing him.

The Torah tells us that the brothers Judah and Reuben tried to save Joseph, but they failed.

Years later, Joseph's love for his family saved the brothers from death.

PLAYING FAVORITES

Joseph was Jacob's favorite son. He gave Joseph a "beautiful coat of many colors." This gift made the brothers angry.

Playing favorites is something everyone hates to see or feel. Many of you have seen a teacher playing favorites with a student. Perhaps a referee or umpire playing favorites with a team. Or perhaps a relative playing favorites with nephews and nieces.

HOW WOULD YOU REACT TO THESE "FAVORITE" SITUATIONS?

1. Your teacher always calls on you with the hardest questions. The other kids always get the easy ones.

   How would you react? _____

2. The referee in the basketball game never calls any fouls on the other team. Your side gets all the foul calls and loses the game.

   How would you react? _____

3. The math genius in the class helps all the other kids. Every time you ask her a question she gives you another excuse for not helping.

   How would you react? _____

71

Joseph and Potiphar

JOSEPH'S BROTHERS HAD sold him as a slave to a caravan on its way to Egypt. In Egypt, Joseph was sold again to a man named Potiphar. Potiphar was captain of the King's guard. Joseph worked hard to please his master.

In a few years, Potiphar made Joseph master of his house. But Potiphar's wife was jealous of Joseph. She was very beautiful, but she was very cruel. She told her husband that Joseph had been rude to her.

"You should have that man thrown into prison," she cried. "After all, he was just a poor slave when you took him in. How dare he be rude to me!"

Potiphar believed the lies his wife told about Joseph. He called the King's guards and told them to throw Joseph into prison.

The keeper of the prison saw that Joseph was a good and kind man.

One day he said:

"I will take off your chains and make you head guard over all the other prisoners."

Joseph spent many hours cheering up these poor men. Prisons in those days were wet and dark. The prisoners were fed very little, and only the very worst kind of food, some of it spoiled and rotten and not fit to eat.

But Joseph kept his mind on the day when God would send him help. He kept thinking of the good things there were in life. At night, as he lay on the hard stone floor of the prison, he would think of his father. He would look at the few stars he could see through the bars across the window and he would think of how beautiful these stars were and how great was the God who created them. These thoughts kept Joseph from dying in the prison. He refused to give up hope.

Joseph In Prison

FOR MANY MONTHS, Joseph was left in the cold, dark prison. But the keeper of the prison had made Joseph guard over all the other prisoners.

One day, two men were led into the prison.

"It is the King's butler and the King's baker," the keeper said to Joseph. "Serve them well!"

One morning, Joseph saw that the butler and the baker looked very sad.

"What is the trouble?" Joseph asked.

"Last night I had a strange dream," said the butler.

"Tell me about it," said Joseph. "Perhaps I can tell you what it means."

"I dreamed I saw a vine, with three branches. On the branches were bunches of grapes. In my hand was the King's cup. I squeezed the juice of the grapes into the cup."

"The three branches are three days," said Joseph. "In three days, the King will send for you to serve him once more as his butler. But when you go back to the palace, remember the poor slave who told you about your dream."

"I, too, had a dream," said the baker. "I dreamed I had three baskets on my head. One basket was filled with bread and cakes for the King. But birds came and ate up the bread and cakes."

Joseph looked very sad; then he said:

"Poor man! The three baskets are three days. In three days, Pharaoh shall hang you from a tree and the birds shall eat your flesh!"

Three days after this, the King sent for the butler to come back to the palace and serve him. But he ordered that the baker should die!

But alas! The butler was so happy to be back at the King's palace that he forgot all about Joseph.

For two more years, Joseph stayed in the dark and lonely prison. But he knew that some day God would help to set him free.

CHOOSE THE CORRECT ANSWER.

1. In prison Joseph was in charge of all the _____.

2. Joseph interpreted the dream of the _____ and the _____ in prison.

3. Joseph's brothers sold him to a caravan on its way to _____.

4. Joseph knew that some day _____ would help to set him free.

5. Joseph was sold to a man called _____.

Potiphar, Egypt, baker, prisoners, butler, God

MATCH THE COLUMNS

A	B
1. Potiphar	His dream meant he would die
2. The baker	King of Egypt
3. The butler	Was sold as a slave
4. Pharaoh	His dream meant he would be freed
5. Joseph	Bought Joseph from the Midianites

WHY did the butler forget about Joseph in prison? **BECAUSE** sometimes people forget the good things that are done for them. Before the butler left prison he promised to help free Joseph. But once out of prison he quickly forgot about Joseph and his promise.

Remembering the good things and being thankful is called gratitude. We recite blessings and prayers of gratitude because we are thankful to God for the good things the Lord has given us and will continue to give us.

You can show gratitude and appreciation to people just by saying "thank you" and remembering your promises.

MAKE SOMEONE HAPPY

Imagine how sad Joseph felt when the butler forgot about him. Because of the butler's forgetfulness Joseph spent another two years in the dark and lonely prison.

I am sure there have been times in your short life when you felt sad just like Joseph. Other times people made you feel angry, happy, and proud.

Tell of a time you made someone else feel that way.

PROUD — Someone made me feel this way when _____

I made someone feel this way when _____

ANGRY — Someone made me feel this way when _____

I made someone feel this way when _____

HAPPY — Someone made me feel this way when _____

I made someone feel this way when _____

SAD — Someone made me feel this way when _____

I made someone feel this way when _____

Joseph and Pharaoh

TWO MORE LONG, dreary years, Joseph remained in the prison. He had almost given up hope, when one day the keeper unlocked the iron door and told him he was to see the great Pharaoh himself.

The Pharaoh had dreamed a dream which greatly troubled him. He had called all the magicians and wise men of his court to tell him what the dreams meant. But he was not satisfied with what they told him. Then the butler remembered the young Hebrew in the prison, and the Pharaoh ordered that Joseph be brought to him at once.

The Pharaoh looked at Joseph curiously when he came into the great throne room. He walked proudly, and his eyes were calm and clear as they looked straight into the eyes of the great Pharaoh of Egypt.

"I like the looks of this man," said the Pharaoh to himself. "He has the mark of a leader." Then he told Joseph what he had dreamed.

"In my dream, I stood by the river and seven fat cows came out of the river and they fed in a meadow. Then seven more cows came up after them, but they were skinny and ill fed and they stood beside the other cows and ate them up. In a second dream I saw seven fat ears of corn; then seven thin ears sprang up beside them and the seven thin ears ate up the seven fat ears."

Joseph said to the mighty Pharaoh:

"I shall tell you what God puts into my mind to say. I think your dreams mean that the seven fat cows are seven good years and the seven lean cows are seven poor ones. And the same with the ears of corn. Egypt shall have seven rich years, but then seven years of terrible famine, when the grain shall wither in the fields. You must set a wise man over Egypt who will store up grain in great storehouses so that when the famine comes there will be food for the people to eat."

The Pharaoh looked at Joseph for a long time. Then he said:

"Since you are so wise, and your God has shown you such wisdom, you surely must be the right man to do this thing. I command you to take charge of the storing of the grain. Indeed, I shall give you the highest office in the land. Only I, the Pharaoh, will be above you."

Then the great Pharaoh took off his gold ring and put it upon Joseph's hand, and gave him clothes of fine linen and put a gold chain around his neck. And Joseph rode in a fine chariot right behind the Pharaoh's own, and the people bowed to him with great respect.

CHOOSE THE CORRECT ANSWER.

1. Pharaoh dreamed a dream that

_____ him.

a. ate

b. troubled

c. remembered

2. The butler remembered the

young _____ in

prison.

a. Egyptian

b. Hebrew

c. baby

3. "Joseph has the mark of a

_____," said the

Pharaoh to himself.

a. leader

b. follower

c. racer

4. "The seven fat cows are seven

good years and the

_____ lean cows are

seven poor years."

a. three

b. five

c. seven

WHO AM I? MATCH THE COLUMNS.

A

1. I am an interpreter of dreams.

2. I am the king of Egypt.

3. I am Joseph's father.

4. I am Joseph's mother.

5. I bought Joseph as a slave.

B

Pharaoh

Joseph

Rachel

Potiphar

Jacob

WHY was Pharaoh troubled by his dream?
BECAUSE in those days people believed that
dreams had special hidden messages. As a matter of
fact, Pharaoh had many dream experts who interpreted
his dreams. The Pharaoh liked Joseph's interpretation of
his dream. Joseph was a good adviser on how to act on
the dream's message.

LET'S PRETEND

Pretend that you are each one of these characters in the story.

Tell about yourself.

How do you feel? What do you think about?

1. I am Joseph. I _____

_____

_____

2. I am the Pharaoh. I _____

_____

_____

3. I am the butler. I _____

_____

_____

Joseph and His Brothers

THE FAMINE WAS so great that it had spread throughout all the land, and even into the land of Canaan where Jacob and his sons lived. Jacob was quite old now and he was worried when he saw that there would be little food to eat. He said to his sons,

"I have heard that there is much corn in Egypt. Go down into Egypt and take money to buy corn, so that we shall not starve."

Joseph's brothers made ready to take the journey to Egypt.

When Joseph's brothers reached Egypt, they were directed to Joseph's great house. You must remember that it had been many years since they had last seen their brother. Joseph had been just a lad when they threw him into the pit. Now he was a man, and he dressed in Egyptian clothes and had learned to speak the Egyptian language. When Joseph saw his brothers walk into the room, he thought surely he would faint.

His brothers did not recognize this great Egyptian lord as the young brother they had left to die in a pit so many years ago.

After the brothers had told Joseph they wanted corn and had money to pay for it, Joseph took a deep breath and said:

"Have you a father and a mother and more brothers at home?"

"Yes, Lord, we have an old father and a younger brother, Benjamin."

"Then prove to me you are not spies," cried Joseph. "Go to your home with your sacks of grain and bring your brother Benjamin here to me."

Some time later the brothers returned and brought Benjamin with them. When Joseph saw Benjamin he could pretend no longer.

"I am Joseph your brother," he cried. "I am Joseph whom you sold as a slave."

The brothers could scarcely believe they had heard right. When they finally realized that this great Egyptian lord was really their long lost brother Joseph, they were afraid. But Joseph said to them:

"Do not fear. I shall not punish you for your sin against me. Don't you see, it was God's will that I come here to Egypt and store up corn so that we all might eat in the time of the famine. But come, make haste to bring my father to me, for I am very homesick to see him!"

Can you imagine Jacob's surprise and joy when the brothers returned home and told him that the Egyptian lord was his own son Joseph! At first the old man did not believe them, but when they showed him the donkeys and the grain and the gifts Jacob wept and thanked God for keeping Joseph alive all those years.

Then Jacob and all his sons and their families went to live in Egypt to be near Joseph, and when Jacob saw his long lost son riding in a beautiful chariot and wearing fine clothes, he wept for joy.

Now Jacob's other name was Israel, and thus it was that the Children of Israel came to live in the land of Egypt.

CHOOSE THE CORRECT ANSWER.

1. "I have heard that there is much

corn in _____."

   a. Alaska

   b. Egypt

   c. Africa

2. "Yes, Lord, we have an old father

and a younger brother,

_____."

   a. Benjamin

   b. Esau

   c. Noah

3. "I am Joseph your brother, whom

you sold as a _____."

   a. slave

   b. actor

   c. toy

4. Then _____ and his

sons and their families went to

live in Egypt.

   a. Jacob

   b. Abraham

   c. Adam

WHO WAS IT? MATCH THE COLUMNS.

A	B
1. Went to Egypt to buy food	Benjamin
2. Father of Joseph	Joseph
3. Joseph's younger brother	Jacob
4. Was sold as a slave	Sons of Jacob

WHY did Joseph forgive his brothers for selling him as a slave?

BECAUSE Joseph saw that his brothers were truly sorry for the way they had treated him. Joseph was a generous person and forgave his brothers for selling him as a slave.

Joseph was happy to share his good fortune with his brothers who were in need.

Joseph made his brothers feel good by forgiving them for selling him as a slave.

FEELING GOOD

The brothers had committed a terrible crime against their brother Joseph. But, Joseph generously forgave his brothers. The brothers felt good after talking to Joseph.

Everybody likes to feel good. List the ways these people make you feel good about who you are and what you do.

My teacher makes me feel good when

1. _____

2. _____

My parents make me feel good when

1. _____

2. _____

My rabbi makes me feel good when

1. _____

2. _____

My friends make me feel good when

1. _____

2. _____

I make myself feel good when

1. _____

2. _____

Birth of Moses

AS LONG AS Joseph lived, and for some time after, the people of Israel were treated kindly by the Egyptians, out of their love for Joseph, who had saved Egypt from suffering by famine. But after a long time, another Pharaoh began to rule over Egypt, who cared nothing for Joseph or Joseph's people. When he saw how the Hebrews were multiplying and prospering, he was afraid they would seize the throne one day and rule all Egypt. Now the Hebrews had no such thought at all. In fact, they were hoping that some day a great leader would come and lead them, to the land that God had promised Abraham, Isaac, and Jacob. The cruel Pharaoh made the Hebrews work as slaves. They carried all the heavy stones that were used to build the Egyptian temples and palaces.

One day, the wicked Pharaoh gave an order to his soldiers.

"There are too many Hebrews in the land of Egypt," he said. "From this day on, you must take every Hebrew boy that is born and throw him into the River Nile to drown."

Soon after this, a baby boy was born. His mother was Jochebed, wife of Amram who belonged to the Hebrew tribe of Levi. Amram and Jochebed had two other children, named Miriam and Aaron. When the new baby was born, Jochebed held him tenderly in her arms.

"How can I let my beautiful little son be thrown into the river?" she cried. "I will hide him so the King's soldiers cannot find him."

For three months, Jochebed kept her baby son hidden. But one day, Miriam and Aaron came running into the house.

"Mother, mother!" they cried. "The King's soldiers are coming!"

Jochebed quickly hid the baby under a pile of clothing. Just then, the soldiers knocked on the door.

"Is there a baby boy in this house?" they cried.

"No!" answered Jochebed. "I have just two children, Miriam and Aaron."

The soldiers looked all over the house, but they did not find the baby.

But Jochebed knew she could not keep her baby hidden forever.

"I shall make a basket of reeds," she said to her husband. "You must patch it with pitch so it will float on the water. I will put our little son into the basket and take it to the river. Perhaps some kind Egyptian family will find our baby."

When Jochebed placed her son in the little basket, her tears fell like rain on his sweet baby face.

"Come," Jochebed said to Miriam, "we will hide the basket in the bulrushes, by the river. Then we will watch and see what happens."

Then the Hebrew mother kissed her son gently, and set the basket boat upon the water. As she watched it float away down the river, she prayed silently.

"Watch over my baby, God," she said. "Somehow, someway, let him grow to be a man."

She watched the little basket until it was out of sight, and then she went sadly back to her house.

COMPLETE THESE SENTENCES.

1. After a long time another _____ began to rule over

_____.

2. The land that God had promised Abraham, _____, and

Jacob.

3. "You must take every _____ boy that is born and throw

him into the Nile _____."

4. Jochebed was the wife of _____.

5. Amram and Jochebed had three children: Miriam, Moses, and

_____.

Aaron, Isaac, Egypt, Pharaoh, River, Hebrew, Amram

WHO WAS IT? MATCH THE COLUMNS.

A	B
1. Amram	Father of Aaron
2. Jochebed	Miriam
3. King of Egypt	Mother of Miriam
4. Brother of Miriam	Pharaoh
5. Sister of Aaron	Aaron

WHY did the new Pharaoh decide to make the Jews of Egypt into slaves?

BECAUSE the new Pharaoh was afraid of the Jews. The old Pharaoh remembered the good things that Joseph had done for Egypt. He also remembered that the Jews were good neighbors and very friendly people.

The new Pharaoh was prejudiced against the Jews.

The word "prejudice" means to dislike a person, a special group, a race of people, or a religion without any reason.

THE HOLOCAUST

The Pharaoh decided to destroy the Jews. When enslavement did not succeed, he ordered that every newborn Hebrew boy be thrown into the Nile River.

Another attempt to destroy the Jews occurred in modern times. In 1933, in Germany, an evil man named *Adolf Hitler* came to power. He and his supporters, the *Nazis,* hated the Jews. They wanted to destroy all the Jews of Europe.

The Nazis fired all the German Jews from their jobs. Jewish children were thrown out of school. Jews were forced to sell their businesses. Some German Jews fled the country; others sent their children to Holland and France.

When World War II began in 1939, the Nazis conquered almost all of Europe. The Jews of the conquered countries fell into their hands. First, they made all Jews wear yellow stars on their clothing. Then they forced the Jews to live in restricted areas called *ghettos.*

Life in the ghettos was very difficult. There wasn't enough food. Often the Nazis turned off the water and the electricity. There were no medicine for the sick. Many Jews died of starvation and disease, but despite the constant fear and hardship, many others managed to survive.

To finish off the remaining Jews as quickly as possible, the Nazis set up *concentration camps*. In these fearful places, millions of Jewish men, women, and children were killed by poison gas.

In Warsaw and other ghettos, brave Jews fought back. Almost unarmed and outnumbered more than ten to one, they inspired the whole world by their courage. Their heroism made all Jews proud. Other Jewish fighters, called *partisans,* kept up the battle even after the ghettos were destroyed. They hid in the countryside and attacked the Germans whenever they could.

When the war ended in 1945, nearly six million Jewish men, women, and children had been killed by the Nazis. We call this event the *Holocaust.* Never in history has one people suffered such a loss. We must always remember their agony and suffering. We must never forget the six million Jews who died during the Holocaust.

OBSERVANCE OF YOM HASHOAH

Many temples observe Yom Hashoah (Holocaust Day) with a special service. In some temples a special six-branched menorah is lit, and memorial prayers are recited.

In Israel, Yom Hashoah is a national day of mourning. An official ceremony takes place at *Yad Vashem,* the Holocaust memorial center in Jerusalem. Everyone in the country observes a moment of silence.

Jews all over the world remember. Non-Jews remember too. All people of good will pray that there will never again be another Holocaust. On Passover we remember the cruel enslavement in Egypt. On Yom Hashoah we remember the Holocaust.

The Egyptian Princess

THE DAUGHTER OF the great Pharaoh of Egypt was walking beside the River Nile with her handmaidens.

"It is such a lovely day," said the princess; "let us walk along the river bank for a while before we go bathing."

Soon they came to a place where tall bulrushes grew beside the river.

"It is the daughter of the great Pharaoh," thought Miriam. "Oh, dear, surely now my little baby brother will be found and killed!"

But Miriam was mistaken. For the Pharaoh's daughter was not like her father. She was as good and kind as she was beautiful. As she dipped her hands into the river, she saw something moving out on the water.

"Look," she cried to her handmaidens. "There is a little basket floating in the water." She sent one of her maids to bring it to her, so that she might see what was in the basket.

The handmaiden brought the basket to her mistress, and when the Princess looked inside, the rosy face of a beautiful baby looked up at her, crying. Pharaoh's daughter's heart was softened, and she held the child close to her.

"Oh, what a beautiful little baby you are," she crooned to it, and when the baby reached up one of its fat little hands and tugged at her lovely long hair, the Princess's eyes filled with tears. "It must be a Hebrew baby."

She was full of pity for the child.

The baby's sister Miriam had crept closer and closer, and she overheard the Princess say these words. She ran forward and cried:

"Your Highness, I know where there is a Hebrew woman who can nurse this child. Shall I call her?"

"Yes, yes, have her come at once," cried the Princess. And so little Miriam ran back to her home and told her mother about the wonderful thing that had happened. The mother was overjoyed. "God has answered my prayer," she cried.

The Princess said to the mother:

"Take the child home and nurse him and I shall pay you good wages for this service."

"I shall call the baby Moses," said the princess, "because this means I drew him from the river."

CHOOSE THE CORRECT ANSWER.

1. "There is a little

_____ floating in the

water."

  a. basket

  b. boat

  c. fish

2. "I shall call the baby

_____," said the

Princess.

  a. Noah

  b. Adam

  c. Moses

3. The daughter of the Pharaoh of

Egypt was walking beside the

_____.

  a. Atlantic Ocean

  b. Nile River

  c. Turnpike

4. The mother said,

"_____ has answered

my prayer."

  a. Moses

  b. God

  c. Pharaoh

MATCH THE RELATIVE. MATCH THE COLUMNS.

A	**B**
1. Mother of Moses	Amram
2. Brother of Miriam	Miriam
3. Father of Moses	Jochebed
4. Sister of Moses	Aaron

WHY did Pharaoh order that every newborn Hebrew boy be thrown into the Nile River to drown?
BECAUSE Pharaoh was afraid of the Hebrews in Egypt. At first the Egyptians tried to kill the Jews with slavery. In spite of the hard work, the number of Jews continued to increase.

So Pharaoh decided to try something new. Pharaoh now decided to murder all the newborn Hebrew boys by drowning them in the river.

HEROES OF HUMANITY

The Princess was a kind Egyptian and had pity on the baby in the basket. She knew that the child was a Hebrew. The Princess also was aware that the Pharaoh had ordered all Hebrew baby boys killed. She placed her own life in danger and saved the Hebrew baby.

In our history, there have been many non-Jewish people who have placed their lives in danger to save Jews.

HERE ARE TWO NON-JEWISH HEROES WHO HELPED HUMAN BEINGS IN TROUBLE:

RAOUL WALLENBERG 1912–1947

Raoul Wallenberg was a Swedish diplomat who saved thousands of Hungarian Jews during World War II.

In 1944 the Swedish government sent Wallenberg to Hungary on a rescue mission. He issued certificates of protection called "Wallenberg passports" to thousands of Jews. These passports saved them from certain death.

In 1944 the Germans rounded up 30,000 Hungarian Jews and forced them to march to an extermination camp. Raoul followed them with a convoy of trucks and distributed food and medicine to the marchers. He even managed to save 500 of the marchers.

At the end of the war Raoul Wallenberg was kidnapped by the Russians and never heard of again. In 1952 the Russians announced that Wallenberg had died in a labor camp in Siberia.

Some believe that Wallenberg is still alive somewhere in Russia.

CHARLES ORDE WINGATE 1903–1944

Born in India into a family of Christian missionaries, Charles Orde Wingate was a deeply religious man. He always carried his Bible with him, so that he could read it whenever he had a spare moment.

Orde was a British army officer who served in Palestine from 1936 to 1939, he became a strong supporter of the Zionist dream to build a Jewish State.

In Palestine, he organized groups of Jewish volunteers, known as Night Squads, to detect and defeat Arab terrorist activities. The Jews called him *Ha-Yedid* — "The Good Friend." But the British disapproved of Wingate's Zionist sympathies and sent him to the Far East. He was killed in Burma during World War II in a plane crash at the age of forty-one.

Wingate remained devoted to the Jewish people and Eretz Yisrael until his tragic death. Israel, in turn, has not forgotten Wingate, and has named a forest, a college of physical education, and a children's village, Yemin Orde, after him.

Moses Fights For The Weak

IN THE PALACE of the Pharaoh of Egypt, there lived the young prince named Moses. But Moses was not a happy prince. The Pharaoh's daughter had treated him like her own son since the day she had found him in the bulrushes when he was a tiny baby. But Moses knew he was a Hebrew, and everywhere he went in the land of Egypt, he saw the Hebrews toiling as slaves.

One day, Moses saw some Hebrews hauling heavy stones along a road. Behind the Hebrews walked an Egyptian with a whip. One of the Hebrews fell down in the road and could not go on.

"Get up, you lazy slave!" cried the Egyptian. Then he began to beat the Hebrew with his whip.

"Stop!" cried Moses. "Can't you see the poor man is too weak to move?"

But the Egyptian kept on beating the Hebrew. Moses became very angry. He struck the Egyptian so hard that the man fell to the ground dead.

"We must hide him in the sand," cried the Hebrew. "If Pharaoh finds out you have killed an Egyptian, he will order your death!"

Moses and the Hebrew hid the dead Egyptian in the sand.

The next day, Moses saw two Hebrews fighting each other in the street.

"Don't you know it is wrong to fight together like that?" Moses cried.

But the men said to him:

"Who are you to tell us not to fight? You, who have killed an Egyptian! Are you going to kill us, too?"

When Moses heard this, he knew his secret had been found out.

"I must leave Egypt and hide in the wilderness," he thought. "For when the Pharaoh finds out I have killed an Egyptian, he will order his soldiers to kill me."

Before Moses left the land of Egypt, he went to say goodby to Jochebed, his mother. Jochebed was an old woman now. Tears ran down her wrinkled cheeks as she kissed her son.

"Do not weep, mother," said Moses. "God will be with me wherever I go. And some day, God will set our people free."

CHOOSE THE CORRECT ANSWER.

1. In the palace of the Pharaoh of Egypt, there lived a young prince named _____.

a. Amram

b. Moses

c. Aaron

2. _____ struck the Egyptian so hard that the man fell to the ground dead.

a. Moses

b. Pharaoh

c. Miriam

3. "When the _____ finds out that I have killed an Egyptian, he will order his soldiers to kill me."

a. Pharaoh

b. Queen

c. Mayor

4. Before Moses left Egypt, he went to say goodbye to _____, his mother.

a. Miriam

b. Jochebed

c. Amram

WHO WAS IT? MATCH THE COLUMNS.

1. King of Egypt   Miriam

2. Mother of Moses   Pharaoh

3. Prince of Egypt   Jochebed

4. Sister of Moses   Moses

WHY did Moses, who was an Egyptian prince, decide to help the Hebrews?

BECAUSE Moses knew that he was a Hebrew. When the Princess found the baby in the basket, she needed someone to care for the tiny boy.

Miriam, the sister of Moses, was hiding in the bushes to see what would happen to her baby brother. Miriam ran up to the Princess and said, "I know where there is a Hebrew woman who can nurse this child." The Princess sent for the woman, who was Jochebed, the baby's mother.

Not only did Jochebed, Moses' own mother, raise him, but she also taught him about God and the people of Israel.

JEWISH LEADERS

Moses was a powerful prince of Egypt. Yet, when he saw a Jew being beaten, he acted bravely.

Moses proved that his love for justice was greater than the power of being an Egyptian prince.

God wanted a powerful person who would lead Israel out of Egypt. By his deeds Moses proved that he was that man.

Here are two Jewish leaders who have led our people in times of trouble:

RABBI LEO BAECK 1873–1956

Leo Baeck was the leader of the Jewish community in Berlin when Hitler came to power.

On the night of November 9, 1938, the Nazis destroyed all the synagogues in Germany. This night of horror is still remembered at Kristallnacht — "the night of the broken glass."

Rabbi Baeck began to hold services in cellars and attics, and even in an empty restaurant. The Nazis arrested him, but because of worldwide pressure, he was soon released.

In 1943 he was arrested again. Now the world was at war, so no one could do anything to help him. He was sent to the Theresienstadt concentration camp.

Leo Baeck organized secret classes in the camp. No matter how tired he was, and no matter how tired and hungry the people were, they went to his inspiring lectures.

In 1945, toward the end of the war, Leo Baeck was sentenced to death. Just in time, Russian soldiers reached the camp. Once again he was a free man.

Leo Baeck influenced the lives of thousands of people all over the world. He taught the value of human life when others wanted to destroy it. He knew the importance of each person in a world where no one seemed to matter.

HENRIETTA SZOLD 1860–1945

Henrietta Szold was born in Baltimore. Her father, a rabbi, believed that girls should be educated as well as boys. He saw to it that Henrietta had a good background in Hebrew and German.

As a young teacher, Henrietta started a school for Jewish immigrants from Russia. A few years later she started the organization now known as Hadassah. It raised money to improve the health conditions of Jews and Arabs in Palestine.

At the age of sixty, Henrietta Szold moved to Palestine. She established a Vocational Training School for Girls in Jerusalem. In 1903, Henrietta Szold set up the Youth Aliyah movement to save the Jewish children of Germany from the Nazis. More than 50,000 children were rescued and settled in Israel.

At Henrietta Szold's funeral, a fifteen-year-old orphan boy recited Kaddish at her graveside. She had no children of her own, but the 50,000 Youth Aliyah children called her Mama. He was one of them.

The Burning Bush

FAR UP ON a hillside, a shepherd was watching his flocks. The shepherd was Moses, and the sheep belonged to his father-in-law.

Moses had fled from Egypt into the Land of Midian. There he had gone to live in the house of Jethro and had married one of Jethro's seven daughters.

But Moses still remembered that his people were slaves in the land of Egypt. As he watched the sheep on the lonely hillside, Moses thought:

"I wish I could do something to help my people."

"Baaaaa!" cried the sheep.

"That's strange," thought Moses. "The sheep seem to be afraid of something."

Then Moses saw a strange sight. Out of a large bush were coming great red flames. But the bush did not burn.

Suddenly, Moses began to tremble, for out of the flames came a voice.

"Moses!" cried the voice. "Take off your shoes, for you are standing upon holy ground!"

Moses took off his shoes and covered his face, for he knew this was the voice of God.

"Moses!" said God, "go and lead thy people out of the land of Egypt."

"I am afraid the people will not believe me when I tell them of this wonderful burning bush! How am I to make them believe that God spoke to me and chose me for their leader?"

"Moses!" commanded God. "Take your rod and throw it on the ground with all your strength!"

Moses was puzzled, but he did as God told him. He threw his rod to the ground. The rod turned into a serpent! Moses turned and ran away from it.

But God called Moses and said:

"Do not be afraid! Put forth your hand and take the serpent by the tail!"

Moses fearfully obeyed. As his hand closed over the snake's tail it became a rod again in Moses' hand!

"Now go to Pharaoh and tell him you will lead the Hebrews out of Egypt," said God. "If the people do not believe you, show them these wonders."

"But they will not listen to me," pleaded Moses, "for I cannot speak well enough."

"Then your brother Aaron will speak for you," said God. "Now go into Egypt! And remember, I will be with you always."

Moses raised his head and looked at the bush. The flames were gone. Then Moses cried out:

"I am not afraid any more, for God is with me. I shall lead my people out of Egypt and into their Promised Land!"

Then Moses began the journey back to Egypt. Little did he dream of the dangers before him, or the hardships he would have to overcome before the Children of Israel found their Promised Land!

COMPLETE THE SENTENCES.

1. Moses had fled from _____ into the land of Midian.

2. Out of a large bush were coming great red _____.

3. "Take off your shoes, for you are standing upon _____ ground."

4. The rod turned into a _____.

5. "Now go to Pharaoh and tell him you will lead the _____ out of Egypt."

6. "I shall lead my people out of Egypt into the _____."

Promised Land, Hebrews, flames, Egypt, holy, serpent

CHOOSE THE CORRECT ANSWER

1. Moses was a _____
   farmer
   shepherd
   King

2. Moses married _____ daughter
   Jethro's
   Pharoah's
   Noah's

3. Moses saw a _____ bush
   burning
   snowy
   electric

4. God said, "Go lead my _____ out of Egypt.
   sheep
   people
   camels

WHY did God speak to Moses from a bush?
BECAUSE God wanted to show Moses that everything in the world, even a lowly little bush, was created by God.

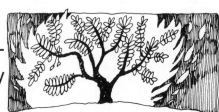

98

BE A REPORTER

Pretend that you are a reporter on the Midianite Times. Your editor has asked you to interview a shepherd called Moses. This shepherd claims that he talked to God. Moses said that God spoke to him from a burning bush and asked him to lead the Jews out of Egypt.

Find out who Moses really is and if he intends to go to Egypt.

Write the story for the newspaper.

Moses Talks To Pharaoh

"GO INTO THE wilderness and meet thy brother Moses!"

These were the words God spoke to Aaron. Now Aaron stood on a mountain top, waiting for his brother. In the distance, he saw a man walking. The man held his head high and in his hand he carried a rod.

"It is Moses, my brother," cried Aaron. When the brothers met, they kissed each other and wept, for they had not seen each other for many years.

Moses told Aaron about the many wonders God had shown him; the burning bush, and the rod turned into a serpent then back into a rod again.

"Now we must go to Pharaoh," said Moses, "and ask him to set our people free."

"There is a new Pharaoh on the throne," said Aaron. "He is very cruel."

"Do not fear, my brother," said Moses. "God is with us."

When they reached Egypt, the brothers gathered together all the families of Israel, and Aaron told them that Moses had been chosen by God to lead them to their Promised Land.

Then Aaron and Moses went to see Pharaoh.

"The God of the Hebrews has sent us to lead the Children of Israel out of Egypt," said Aaron.

Pharaoh's eyes were cold and cruel.

"I know nothing of your God. Who is this God? Show me some of your God's wonders," said Pharaoh.

Aaron threw his rod upon the ground and it became a serpent.

"My magicians can do that much!" laughed Pharaoh. He called his magicians and told them to cast their rods upon the ground. The rods all turned into serpents. But quick as a wink, Aaron's rod ate up all the other rods.

Pharaoh became very angry.

"Get out of my sight!" he cried to Moses and Aaron. "And from this day on, the Hebrews will work harder than ever. They will not only make the bricks to build our temples — they will have to find the straw to put into the bricks!"

Moses and Aaron fled from the palace. Their hearts were heavy. Moses prayed.

"What have I done, O Lord?" he cried. "Now my people work harder than ever!"

"Do not fear, Moses," said God. "For I am with you always. The Egyptians will soon find out about the God of the Children of Israel!"

CHOOSE THE CORRECT ANSWER.

1. "Go to the wilderness and meet

your _____."

   a. mother

   b. brother Moses

   c. train

2. Aaron told the Israelites that

Moses would lead them into

_____.

   a. the Promised Land

   b. the movies

   c. Egypt

3. The Pharaoh said, "Show me

some of God's

_____."

   a. children

   b. wonders

   c. animals

4. Aaron's rod ate up all the

_____.

   a. other rods

   b. sandwiches

   c. cookies

WHO DID IT? MATCH THE COLUMNS.

A	B
1. Fled from Egypt	God
2. Saw a burning bush	Pharaoh
3. He and Moses went to Pharaoh	Moses
4. Was King of Egypt	Aaron
5. Spoke to Moses from a bush	Moses

WHY did Moses take his brother, Aaron, with him to Pharaoh's palace?
BECAUSE Moses was a stutterer and was ashamed to speak in public.

God said to Moses: "You will speak to Aaron and tell him what to say. I will help both of you to know what to say and what to do."

First, God would speak to Moses. Then Moses would tell Aaron what to say.

102

HOW WOULD YOU HELP?

As you go through life you will meet all kinds of people. Some of them will be handicapped. There are all kinds of handicaps. Some handicapped people, like Moses, are stutterers. Some of them have difficulty walking, running, or jumping.

Sometimes, and this is true among older people, the handicapped cannot see or hear well. And sometimes people are handicapped with a sickness that makes them act differently.

Of course, we don't tease or make fun of them because of their problems. As a matter of fact, Jewish law says that it is a mitzvah to help handicapped people. We call this mitzvah Gemilat Chasadim.

HOW COULD YOU DO THE MITZVAH OF GEMILAT CHASADIM IN THESE SITUATIONS?

1. You see a person with a cane trying to climb some steps. _____
   _____

2. You see a person trying to read the street sign or a name on the bulletin board. _____
   _____

3. There is a kid in the class who has a hearing handicap. _____
   _____

The Ten Plagues

"HOW SHALL I help my people, O Lord," prayed Moses. "The Pharaoh is making them work harder than ever!"

"Ask Pharaoh again to set your people free," said God. "If he will not, then stretch out your rod over the river and the Egyptians will know I am the Lord!"

The next day, Pharaoh was standing beside the River Nile. Many of his people were gathered around him.

"My God commands that you set the Hebrews free," said Moses to Pharaoh.

"I told you I know nothing of your God!" cried Pharaoh.

"Then you shall know him!" said Moses.

He stretched his rod over the waters of the Nile. Suddenly, the Egyptians began screaming with fear. The waters of the great river had turned to blood! Every fish in the river was dead!

For seven days the Nile was a river of blood. The Egyptians were dying of thirst. Then the river became clear.

After this Moses spoke to Pharaoh.

"Now if you do not set my people free, the Lord will send thousands of frogs into your land."

But Pharaoh would not let the Hebrews go.

Then came the frogs.

"Tell your God to take them away!" cried Pharaoh. "I will let the Hebrews go!"

The frogs died, but Pharaoh did not keep his promise.

Then God sent millions of lice to bite the Egyptians. Even the great Pharaoh scratched and scratched until he could bear it no longer.

"Tell your God to take away the lice!" he cried. But when the lice were gone, Pharaoh still said, "No!"

Then came the wild beasts. Then a terrible sickness that killed all the cattle. Then the bodies of the Egyptians broke out with boils. They itched all over and spent their days scratching themselves. Hail came and spoiled the crops. Locusts ate up what was left of the crops. Then came a terrible darkness that lasted for three days. But still Pharoah would not let the Hebrews go.

"Let the firstborn of every Egyptian die!" said God.

Then came a time of weeping and sadness, for the firstborn son of every Egyptian family lay dead. Pharaoh's head was bowed with grief, for he, too, had lost his firstborn son.

"Take your flocks and your people," he cried to Moses, "and go from the Land of Egypt."

Pharaoh had learned at last that the power of God is greater than the power of the greatest king.

CHOOSE THE CORRECT ANSWER.

1. "Ask Pharaoh to set your

_____."

　　a. people free

　　b. hair

　　c. clocks

2. The waters of the great river had

turned into _____.

　　a. ice

　　b. blood

　　c. stars

3. "Let the _____ of

every Egyptian die."

　　a. dog

　　b. firstborn

　　c. wife

4. "I told you I know nothing of your

_____!"

　　a. butcher

　　b. doctor

　　c. God

5. Then came a terrible

_____ that lasted

three days.

　　a. earthquake

　　b. darkness

　　c. movie

WHY did God choose to punish the Egyptians with plagues?

BECAUSE, the Rabbis say, the plagues were God's revenge for the cruelty of the Egyptians against the Jews.

Because the Jews were forced to carry water for the Egyptians, the water turned into blood.

Because the Egyptians forced the Jews to catch fish for them, the rivers were filled with frogs.

Because the Egyptians murdered the boy-children of the Jews, God sent the tenth plague, which killed the young Egyptian boys.

FIND THE PLAGUES

Find the Ten Plagues among the mixed up letters. Look for them by reading forwards, down, and on the diagonal. The words are always on a straight line. Some words may overlap.

```
B Y B C D E F E G Y I J K C M M
A L A B C Z Y C L Z H X F W V O
B D O K J D A A U S Z A L A U P
C F R O G S B T V T A X I B T Q
D E O L D E C T W L B W E L S R
E F P M I F Z L B O I L S D R S
F G Q N H G Y E X C C V R E Q T
G H L M N O P D Q U D U L F P U
H I K J I H G I F S E T S I O V
I J R Q P O M S M T L K J M C W
J K D A R K N E S S I H G L M E
K L A B C D E A F G H I J K Z X
L M N O P Q R S S T U V W X Y Y
M N O P Q R S E T U V W X Y Z Z
D E A T H O F F I R S T B O R N
```

BLOOD, FROGS, FLIES, BOILS, HAIL, LOCUSTS, DARKNESS, CATTLE DISEASE, DEATH OF FIRST-BORN, LICE

Crossing The Red Sea

SUDDENLY, EARLY IN the morning, the Israelites went out of the land after more than 200 years in Egypt. They went out in order, like a great army, family by family and tribe by tribe, after joyfully gathering everything they owned, even the bread which had been started that evening, but which didn't have time to rise. Because the Children of Israel took that flat, unleavened bread, matzoh, with them out of Egypt, unleavened bread is still eaten at Passover time, in memory of that day when Moses led his people out of slavery. Marching ahead of them was their great leader, Moses. And God sent a pillar of cloud to lead them by day, and a pillar of fire by night.

But back in the land of Egypt, Pharaoh was wishing he had not let the Hebrews go. For now the Egyptians had to do all the hard work. Pharaoh called one of his captains to him and said:

"Which way did the Hebrews go?"

"They are marching toward the Red Sea," said the captain.

"They will never be able to cross it," said Pharaoh. "Send an army after the Hebrews at once. We must have our slaves back again!"

Tramp, tramp, tramp, marched the Children of Israel.

Gallop-a-gallop-a-gallop came the Egyptian army behind them.

When the Hebrews reached the Red Sea, they heard the sound of galloping horses.

"The Egyptians!" cried the Children of Israel. "They have come after us!"

Then they cried to Moses:

"You have led us into the wilderness to be killed like dogs!"

Moses bowed down and asked God to help him.

"Stretch out your rod over the water," said God. Lo and behold! When Moses stretched his rod over the Red Sea, the waters parted and left a path of dry land. With a joyful shout, Moses led the Children of Israel across to the other side.

When the Egyptians saw them marching into the sea, they followed with their chariots and their horses. But the sand was no longer hard; it had become soft, and their chariot wheels were caught in it. Many wheels broke off the chariots. And the horses sank in the mud and fell down, so that the army was in confusion, and all were frightened.

By this time, all the Israelites had passed through the Red Sea and were standing on the high ground beyond it, looking at their enemies slowly struggling through the sand, all in one heaped-up mass of men and horses and chariots. Then Moses lifted up his hand, and at once a great tide of water swept up from the sea on the south; the road over which the Israelites had walked in safety was covered with water; and the host of Pharaoh, with all his chariots and his horses and their riders, were drowned in the sea, before the eyes of the people of Israel.

Safe on the other side, Moses and the Children of Israel bent their heads and thanked God for helping them.

Because of God's miracles in Egypt we celebrate the holiday of Passover.

CHOOSE THE CORRECT ANSWER.

1. The Children of Israel took _____ with them out of Egypt.

2. God sent the _____ to lead them out of Egypt.

3. "They are marching toward the _____," said the captain.

4. "Send an army after the _____ at once."

5. With a joyful shout Moses led the _____ across to the other side.

Children of Israel, matzoh, Children of Israel, Red Sea, Pillar of Cloud

MATCH THE COLUMNS.

A	B
1. unleavened bread	Sea
2. Pillar of Cloud	day
3. Pillar of Fire	Hebrew leader
4. Moses	night
5. Red	matzah

WHY do we give Tzedakah before Passover?

BECAUSE Passover reminds us of the suffering of our people in Egypt long ago.

Tzedakah means "charity." We do Tzedakah when we help the poor and those who cannot help themselves.

Right after the holiday of Purim, the synagogues and the temples begin collecting Tzedakah for the holiday of Pesach.

This special Tzedakah money is called Maot Chittim ("money for wheat").

Years ago Maot Chittim money was used to buy wheat. This wheat was baked into matzah for poor people.

It is a mitzvah to share with others and to help them. Helping and sharing is something God wants us to do. If we share with other people, we are helping make the world a better place in which to live.

Sometimes, we do not know any people to help. Synagogues and temples collect the Maot Chittim money and buy food, clothing, and medicine for people who need it.

THE SEDER PLATE

In the center of the Seder table you place a special plate called a **Karah.** The **Karah** has five special symbols. Each of these symbols tells us something about the holiday of Passover.

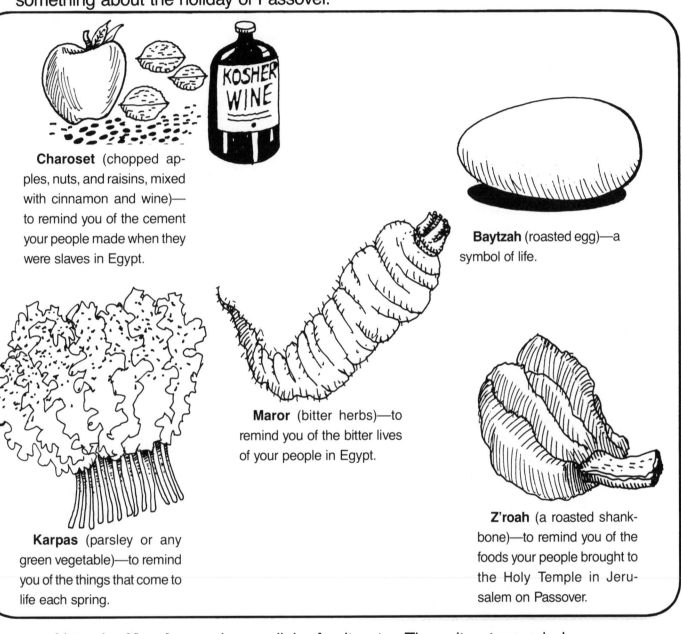

Charoset (chopped apples, nuts, and raisins, mixed with cinnamon and wine)—to remind you of the cement your people made when they were slaves in Egypt.

Baytzah (roasted egg)—a symbol of life.

Maror (bitter herbs)—to remind you of the bitter lives of your people in Egypt.

Karpas (parsley or any green vegetable)—to remind you of the things that come to life each spring.

Z'roah (a roasted shankbone)—to remind you of the foods your people brought to the Holy Temple in Jerusalem on Passover.

Near the **Karah,** we place a dish of salt water. The salt water reminds us of the tears of our people in Egypt.

WHY do we eat matzoh on Passover.?
BECAUSE matzoh was the poor bread the Jews ate as they left Egypt.

Matzoh also reminds us of people all over the world who are still in slavery.

Matzoh also reminds us of people everywhere who are poor and hungry.

Manna From Heaven

FAR INTO THE wilderness marched the Children of Israel. Wherever they stopped they built leafy huts to protect them from the hot desert sun. They called these huts "sukkot". No longer did they sing a joyful song, for their food was gone and they were very hungry. The hot sun beat down upon them. The children cried for water.

"We were better off in Egypt," cried some of the Hebrews. "At least we had food to eat and water to drink."

When Moses heard these words, he said:

"We must be brave and trust in the Lord. He will send us food."

On and on they marched. At last they came to a bubbling stream of water Marah. The word "Marah" means "bitter". But the water just like the name was bitter and the people could not drink it.

Then God told Moses to put a special tree into the water, and the water became sweet. How good it tasted to the thirsty travelers!

But still the Children of Israel grumbled, for they had no food.

Again Moses prayed to God for help.

Suddenly, from the pillar of cloud that was leading them, came the voice of God!

"You will suffer no more," said God. "At evening you will have meat to eat. In the morning, I will rain down bread from heaven."

Just as the sun went down at the end of that day, a flock of quail flew over the Hebrews' camp.

"It is the meat God promised us!" cried Moses. They caught the birds and cooked them. They tasted better than anything the Hebrews had even eaten!

The next morning, the Children of Israel saw upon the ground tiny white things that looked like bread crumbs.

"It is the bread God promised us!" cried Moses.

The Hebrews tasted the little white crumbs.

They had never seen anything like it before and they said, just as anybody would say, "What is it?" In the language of the Israelites, the Hebrew language, "What is it?" is the word "manhu." So the people said to one another "Man hu? Man hu?" And this gave a name afterward to what they saw, the name *Manna.*

And Moses said to them, "This is the bread which the Lord has given you to eat. Go out and gather it, as much as you need. But take only as much as you need for today, for it will not keep, and God will give you more tomorrow."

Some of the people were greedy and gathered more. But the next day it was sour and spoiled.

Every day, for five days, the Children of Israel gathered the manna and ate it. But on the sixth day, Moses said:

"Today you must gather enough manna for two days. Tomorrow is the Sabbath and there will be no manna."

On the sixth day, the Hebrews gathered enough manna for two days, and the next day it was not spoiled.

On the Sabbath day, the Hebrews prayed to God and thanked the Lord for sending them food and water in the wilderness.

CHOOSE THE CORRECT ANSWER.

1. "Tomorrow is the

_____ and there will

be no manna."

a. Sabbath

b. Hanukah

c. Rosh Hashanah

2. Moses put a certain tree into the

water and the water became

_____ .

a. sweet

b. sour

c. Coca-Cola

3. "At evening you will have

_____ to eat."

a. pizza

b. potatoes

c. meat

4. " 'What is it?' is the word

'_____ .' "

a. Israel

b. manhu

c. Shalom

5. _____ , the Children

of Israel gathered the manna and

ate it.

a. six hours

b. one year

c. five days

6. "We were better off in

_____ ."

a. Israel

b. Egypt

c. America

WHY did the Jews build sukkot in the desert?
BECAUSE the desert was very hot and they
needed protection from the sun. The sukkot were built
out of leafy branches that they found in the desert. The
green branches shaded them from the rays of the hot
sun.

At night, as they lay in their leafy sukkot, they could
see millions of stars twinkling in the sky. They felt safe
because they knew that God was watching over them.

These very same stars twinkle for us too. We too feel
safe, because we know that the God that watched over
the Jews in the desert is also protecting us.

THE HOLIDAY OF SUKKOT

Five days after Yom Kippur, the holiest day of the Jewish year, comes one of the happiest of all festivals. It is called Sukkot, which means "booths" or "tabernacles."

In the history of every people there are great moments which it likes to recall in order to be reminded of the past and to learn from the past a lesson for the future.

After our ancestors left Egypt, the Bible tells us, they wandered for forty years in the desert before they reached the Promised Land. During all these years they lived in sukkot (booths) made of dry palms and such branches as they could find. The Bible tells us to dwell in sukkot seven days each year in remembrance of the years of wandering and hardship.

After our forefathers had settled in Canaan, they discovered that the autumn, when Sukkot was celebrated, was also the time when they gathered in the crops. So Sukkot became a double celebration. We were grateful that we were no longer wanderers in the desert; and we offered thanks to God for the gathering-in of the crops. Thus Sukkot became the Jewish Thanksgiving.

Did you know that there is a close connection between our American holiday of Thanksgiving and the Jewish festival of Sukkot?

In the fall of 1621 the settlers in Plymouth colony gathered to give thanks to God for a bountiful harvest after their first hard year in the New World. That was America's first Thanksgiving.

Where did the early Pilgrims get the idea for a Thanksgiving Day? They were religious men and women. The book they loved most dearly was the Bible. Many of their laws and customs were based on the Bible, and they gave their children Biblical names like Ezekiel, Moses, Solomon, and Hannah.

The Pilgrims also knew of the festival of Sukkot, and the Biblical command: *"When you have gathered in the fruits of the land, you shall keep the feast of the Lord"* (Leviticus 23:39).

So we can be certain that the Pilgrims drew their inspiration for Thanksgiving from the Bible. Thus, the spirit of the Bible, as well as Jewish history and custom, were all expressed in the first Thanksgiving celebrated by the Pilgrims in the autumn of 1621.

The most important symbol of Sukkot is the *sukkah* itself. The sukkah is a small hut or booth. Often it is made of boards nailed together. Sometimes it is prefabricated and kept from year to year. It is just sturdy enough to be used for a few days and offers no real protection against wind or rain. There is no permanent roof. Instead, leafy branches are thrown loosely over the top. From inside the sky can be seen.

The sukkah is a reminder of the temporary shelters used by the Jews in ancient times. Just as those shelters did not protect against the elements, so too must the sukkah be built so that it does not protect against the elements.

In our time most sukkot are built in the courtyards of temples. The worshippers stop in after services to eat some refreshments and recite the special blessings that are said in the sukkah. But many families have their own sukkah. They build it themselves and have all their meals there for the entire festival. Some Jews even sleep in the sukkah.

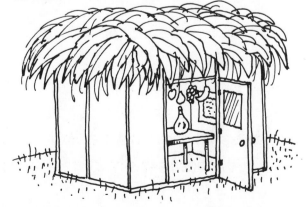

The Ten Commandents

AS THEY WANDERED on and on, there were times when Moses thought he would have to give up. Sometimes fierce desert tribes attacked their camp during the night. But the men of Israel always drove these wild desert warriors away.

One day, three months after they had left Egypt, the Children of Israel came to the wilderness of Sinai. They made camp at the foot of a great mountain.

"Let us make camp here at the foot of the mountain," said Moses.

Late that night, when the campfires were glowing embers, and the Children of Israel lay sleeping, Moses stood alone under the bright stars. Suddenly he heard the voice of God saying:

"Moses, go alone to the mountain top and receive My great laws."

The next morning, Moses spoke to the people.

"I must leave you for a while. God has told me to go alone to the top of the mountain. My brother Aaron will take my place while I am gone."

Then Moses started up the mountain. The way was very steep. It was dark night when he reached the top. Then Moses cried out:

"Lord, I have come to receive Your commandments."

No sooner had he spoken than a flash of lightning came out of the sky. Thunder rolled from the heavens like the beating of a hundred drums. Moses heard the voice of God.

"These are My great Commandments," said God.

"I am the Lord your God.

You shall have no other gods before Me!

You shall not take the name of the Lord in vain.

Remember the Sabbath to keep it holy.

Honor your father and your mother.

You shall not murder.

You shall not be unfaithful.

You shall not steal.

You shall not bear false witness.

You shall not want what is your neighbor's."

God then gave Moses two tablets of stone on which the Ten Commandments were written.

Suddenly the lightning stopped flashing. The thunder rolled no more. All was still on the mountain top.

Then Moses started down the mountain with the two tablets of stone to tell the people about the Ten Commandments.

Thousands of years have passed since God gave Moses the Ten Commandments, and all the nations of the world know these laws.

If everyone always remembered these laws and obeyed them, what a wonderful world this would be!

COMPLETE THE SENTENCE.

1. The Children of Israel came to the wilderness of _____.

2. "My brother _____ will take my place while I am gone."

3. Moses heard the voice of _____.

4. God gaves Moses two _____ of stone.

5. No better _____ have ever been written.

6. "Lord, I have come to receive Your _____."

commandments, God, Sinai, Aaron, tablets, laws

THE COMMANDMENTS   COMPLETE THE SENTENCE.

1. Remember the _____ to keep it holy.

2. You shall not _____.

3. You shall not want what is your_____.

4. Honor your father and your_____.

5. You shall not bear false _____.

6. I am the Lord, thy _____.

7. You shall not take the name of the _____ in vain.

Lord, witness, steal, Sabbath, neighbor's, mother, God

WHY is Shavuot known as the "Season of the Giving of the Law"?
BECAUSE it was at that time that the Law—the Ten Commandments—was given to the Jews.

The Rabbis say that Torah was also revealed at Mount Sinai on Shavuot.

THE BIBLE

The Latin word *Bible* means "book". But the Bible is really a collection of books all in one book. It is a "library" of books holy to our people.

Our most cherished possession, the Bible, has been translated from Hebrew into over a thousand languages. It continues today, as in ages past, to help people lead a righteous life. The Bible tells us that there is One God; it teaches us to honor our parents; it urges us to tell only the truth. The Bible contains the world's most wonderful stories—of heroic people like Moses, Joshua, Deborah, and Samson; of important events like the Flood and the Exodus; of stirring prophecies like those of Isaiah and Jeremiah.

For us, the Bible—especially the Torah—has been the very center of Jewish life. Study it over and over again, said the Rabbis, for all knowledge and wisdom may be found in it.

The Bible consists of thirty-nine books divided into three sections: The *Torah,* the *Prophets,* and the *Writings.*

The *Torah* consists of the first five books of the Bible, called the Five Books of Moses. The stories in this book are from the Torah. The names of the Five Books of Moses in Hebrew are: Bereshit, Shmot, Vayikrah, Bamidbar, Devarim.

WHY did God give the Torah to the Jews?

BECAUSE God first offered the Torah to other nations and they refused it.

Before giving the Torah to the Israelites, God offered it to various other nations of the world. "Will you accept and obey My Torah?" God asked the first nation.

"What does it say?" they asked.

"It says 'You shall not kill,' " answered God.

"We cannot accept and obey the Torah," answered the first nation. "Throughout our history we have lived by the sword."

Then God asked the second nation, "Will you accept and obey My Torah?"

"What does it say?" they asked.

"It says 'Honor your father and your mother,' " answered God.

"We cannot accept and obey the Torah," answered the second nation. "We reject our parents when they grow old."

God asked all the nations of the world. But none would promise to accept and obey the Torah. Then God asked Israel. The Israelites did not ask what was in the Torah. They did not hestitate. They answered, "All that God has spoken we will do and we will obey."

The Golden Calf

MOSES HAD LEFT the Children of Israel and gone to the top of Mount Sinai. The people began grumbling to each other.

"Perhaps he will never come back!" some of them said.

"Moses will come back," said Aaron. "You must trust in God."

Finally, some of the people went to Aaron and said:

"Moses has not returned. Perhaps he never will. We need a god to worship. We want someone to lead us! Give us a god who will tell us what to do!"

You see, while the Children of Israel had lived in Egypt, they had seen the Egyptians worshiping statues of animals and all sorts of idols made of stone and metal. They felt lost without something to kneel to, and their faith was not yet strong enough to trust in their one true God. They wanted something they could see!

Aaron saw that the people were restless and ready to start trouble.

"Very well," said Aaron, "I will make you a god if you must have something to worship. Bring me your gold jewelry and your gold rings."

Then Aaron built a hot fire and put all the gold rings and jewelry into it. The people watched as their gold melted and became a mass of hot metal. Then Aaron shaped this liquid gold into a calf. He set the Golden Calf upon its feet and said:

"There is the god you asked for! Now let him lead you out of the wilderness!"

The people cried aloud with joy, for they foolishly believed this metal animal that had no life at all, nor a mind nor a soul, was their god!

"Stop!" cried a voice like thunder. The Children of Israel stood still, trembling with fear. Standing before them was Moses. In his hands he held the two stone tablets on which had been written the laws of God. Moses' eyes flashed with anger. He threw the stone tablets to the ground and they crashed to bits. Then he picked up the golden calf and threw it into the fire. When it had melted into a ball, he ground the ball to powder under his foot. He threw the powder into the water and said to the people:

"Drink this water!"

Then Moses cried out to Aaron:

"Why did you let the people do this wicked thing?"

"I was afraid they would kill me," said Aaron.

"Are there any of you who have not forgotten the Lord?" Moses asked.

The men of the tribe of Levi came and stood beside him. Then Moses asked God to forgive the people.

"Lead the people from this place," said God. "I will send an angel before you."

Then God told Moses to go to the top of Mount Sinai again to receive two more tablets of stone. For forty days and forty nights, Moses stayed on the mountain top. When he came down, the Children of Israel were waiting for him. Moses gave his people the Ten Commandments. The Children of Israel bowed their heads and promised God they would always try to obey His great laws.

CHOOSE THE CORRECT ANSWER.

1. For forty days and

_____ Moses stayed

on the mountain top.

   a. forty nights

   b. thirty days

   c. five months

2. In his hands Moses held the Ten

_____.

   a. Commandments

   b. draydels

   c. shofars

3. "Bring me your gold

_____ and your gold

rings."

   a. hamburgers

   b. toys

   c. jewelry

4. Moses left the Children of Israel

and climbed to the top of

_____.

   a. Mount America

   b. Mount Sinai

   c. Mount Ararat

MATCH THE COLUMNS.

1. Children of	calf
2. golden	Israel
3. Mount	tablets
4. Ten	Sinai
5. stone	Commandments
6. tribe of	Levi

WHY did Aaron help make the Golden Calf?
BECAUSE, the Rabbis say, Aaron was a weak
man and surrendered to the mob. Aaron tried to explain
and communicate to the people that a golden calf could
not be a god. It was just plain stupid to think that an
animal could be a god. The mob refused to listen so he
surrendered and helped make the idol. He melted down
the gold and helped make the golden calf.

Moses had disappeared for forty whole days. Perhaps, Aaron was just trying to calm the Hebrews till his
brother Moses returned.

COMMUNICATION AND YOU

The most famous story about communication is the Tower of Babel. God mixed up the language of the builders so that the people could not go on planning and working together.

The ancient Hebrews understood the power of language and communication. The most important idea about language is that without it people cannot communicate and exchange ideas to build great things and to live in a peaceful world.

Each of you thinks and has your own ideas. Unless you can tell or communicate your ideas, no own will ever know about them. Just as a person cannot live without breathing, humanity cannot exist without language and communication.

Communication is the breath of life for the human race. Just imagine, a spaceship has landed in your backyard. The ramp goes down and an alien exits. Of course, the alien cannot speak English or Hebrew, and you, naturally, cannot speak alienese.

How would you communicate these ideas to the person from outer space? Use drawings, sign language, words, computer language.

1. You are peaceful and mean no harm. _____
   _____

2. You wish to invite it to your house for supper. _____

   _____
   _____

3. You want the alien to go to school with you. _____
   _____
   _____

4. You would like to learn about where the alien came from and how it got to Earth. _____

   _____

5. Suppose foreigners moved into the house next door. Would you use the same techniques to get to know them? _____
   _____
   _____

The Holy Ark

AFTER MOSES BROUGHT down the tablets of stone from Mount Sinai, with the laws of God carved upon them, the children of Israel said to one another:

"Now we have God's own laws to guide us and tell us what is right and what is wrong.

"We also need a holy place in which to pray."

God said to Moses:

"Have the people build a Holy Tent, or Tabernacle, which will be carried with you as you journey to the Promised Land. Build this Tabernacle very carefully. Let everyone help, every man and woman and even the small children. Decorate the Tabernacle with gold and fine linen.

"Place the sacred tablets within the Ark. Then put the Ark in the center of the Tabernacle and before it hang a veil. This shall be your Holy of Holies."

Every man and woman began at once to do his or her part to help build the Holy of Holies. The men engraved shining gold, the women wove fine linens, and the children held the rolls of flax or carried things back and forth to help.

When the tent was finished, it was covered with curtains and goats' hair and rams' skins which had been dyed red. Inside the tent the people hung ten curtains of blue and purple and bright scarlet. Now it was time to build the Holy Ark.

The Ark was built with great care by the finest carpenter, Bezalel. He was a great artist and taught the people how to make everything as beautiful as possible.

At last the Ark was finished. Very carefully Moses lifted the Holy Ark and carried it into the Tabernacle.

The Children of Israel all gathered in front of the Tabernacle to look at the beautiful work they had done. They were very proud, and well they might be! The gold glistened in the sun. The beautiful red and gold and purple colors of the curtains were like a glorious rainbow. There was not a man, woman, or child who had not worked hard to make the Holy of Holies a beautiful and perfect place.

Moses held up his hand, and everyone was very still. Then Aaron, the High Priest, came forward, carrying the sacred tablets. He wore the dazzling breast plate, the ephod. Twelve sparkling jewels set into it, each jewel bearing the name of a different tribe of Israel. Aaron stepped inside the Holy of Holies, and Moses spoke to the people:

"Our work is done and our Holy of Holies is beautiful. We now have a holy place in which to pray.

Then the Children of Israel gave thanks to God, and the Levites played holy music and sang hymns of praise. Aaron, the High Priest, brought the sacred tablets inside the Holy of Holies.

CHOOSE THE CORRECT ANSWER.

1. "Place the sacred tablets within

the _____."

a. safe

b. car

c. Ark

2. Aaron, the _____,

came forward, carrying the

sacred tablets.

a. Egyptian

b. High Priest

c. artist

3. _____, one of the

Children of Israel, was a great

artist.

a. Aaron

b. Bezalel

c. Moses

4. The ephod had twelve jewels set

in it, each jewel bearing the name

of a different _____.

a. tribe of Israel

b. river in Egypt

c. city in America

MATCH THE COLUMNS

A	B
1. Breastplate	Sinai
2. Aaron	ephod
3. Bezalel	Holy Tent
4. Holy of	High Priest
5. Tabernacle	artist
6. Desert	Holies

WHY did all the Jews, big and small, want to help build the Tabernacle?

BECAUSE everyone was grateful for God's miracle.

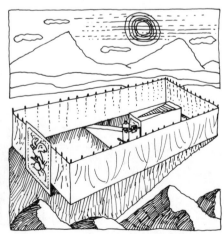

They showed their faith and their love for God by helping build the Tabernacle.

God saved them from slavery in Egypt. The Lord sent them manna and quail when they were hungry. And it was God who gave them water to drink.

YOUR SYNAGOGUE

No one was forced to work or to give for the building of the Tabernacle. But, all of our ancestors gave willingly. They gave gold and silver and materials of all kinds. They also gave their labor. Even the small children helped by running errands and cleaning up.

The Tabernacle was a beautiful House of Worship which accompanied the Hebrews through all their years of wandering in the desert.

People can pray to God in any place — at home, at play, in someone's house and in the Synagogue or Temple. But, just as it is good to live together with other people, it is good to pray together with other people. In the Synagogue you pray with your fellow Jews. The Synagogue is your house of prayer.

Your beautiful Synagogue was built by people who love God and Judaism. They willingly gave their time and their money to build your beautiful Temple.

YOUR SYNAGOGUE FACTS

1. Name of your Synagogue _____
2. Address of your Synagogue _____
3. Your Synagogue was built in _____
4. Your Rabbi's name is _____
5. Your Cantor's name is _____
6. Your Principal's name is _____
7. Your teacher's name is _____
8. What do you like about your Synagogue? _____

_____

9. How can you make your Synagogue a better place? _____

_____

Spies To Canaan

THE CHILDREN OF Israel had reached the wilderness of Paran. Just beyond the mountains lay their Promised Land.

"Is it really a land of milk and honey?" the people wondered.

"We must send scouts to find out," said Moses. Then he called the men of Israel together.

"There must be one scout from each tribe," he said. "There will be much danger."

Each of the tribes chose one scout for the dangerous mission. There were 12 scouts in all.

The next morning, Moses said to the scouts:

"Go southward through the mountains into the Land of Canaan. Find out how many people live there and what they are like. When you return, bring back some of the fruit of the land."

The scouts started on their journey. After many weary days, they came to a pass in the mountains. Below them was a beautiful green valley:

"Let us go down and see what it is like," said Joshua. But when they reached the cities, they found guards outside, and the spies were cautious about entering.

"The people all look like giants!" said one of the spies.

"Let us go back!" said another. The spies picked some figs and a huge stalk of grapes and pomegranates to take back to Moses. When they returned to their camp in the wilderness, the people cried out with joy. Then their questions came pouring forth:

"Is there lots of grass?"

"Are there plums and pomegranates and other fruit?"

"Is there plenty of water?"

"Are the people tall or short?"

Moses smiled and held up his hand.

"One at a time," he said. "First of all, what of the people of this new land? Are they friendly?"

Ten of the spies looked very serious, and they shook their heads.

"No," they answered, "they are not friendly at all. They are very fierce and warlike. Their cities have great high walls around them."

But Caleb said quickly:

"What do these things matter to the brave Children of Israel, who have already fought the wilderness! Besides, we have God on our side. We must go and fight these fierce people and claim our rightful homeland."

But the people were afraid.

"Why did you bring us from our homes in Egypt?" they cried to Moses. "Now we will be killed by giants!"

"Silence!" cried Moses. "This land is not for you! You are not brave enough! For forty years you must wander in the wilderness. You will never see the Promised Land. But your children will have courage! They will come back and march into the Promised Land without you!"

And so began forty years of wandering for the Children of Israel.

WHO SAID IT? CHOOSE THE CORRECT ANSWER.

1. "Is it really a land of milk and honey?" _____

2. "We must send scouts to find out." _____

3. "I will go!" _____

4. "What do these things matter to the brave Children of Israel?"

_____

5. "This land is not for you!" _____

the people, Moses, Joshua, Caleb, Moses

WHY was there a difference of opinions among the twelve spies?

BECAUSE sometimes people can look at the same movie, game, or concert and feel differently about it.

Ten of the men looked and feared the enemy.

Joshua and Caleb refused to be part of the majority. Joshua and Caleb were not afraid. They were strong enough to stand up and state their own differing opinion.

130

THE STATE OF ISRAEL

Jacob, who was renamed Israel by the angel, dreamed of a return to Canaan, the land of his birth. Today, the land of Canaan is called the State of Israel.

The Torah tells us that long, long ago the Land of Israel was "a land flowing with milk and honey." The Torah also tells us that the Jews of ancient Israel were very good farmers. They plowed their fields and planted grain and fruit trees. In their vineyards, great luscious clusters of grapes hung from the vines. The sheep in the fields of ancient Israel were fat and healthy and had lots of rich, green grass to eat. Mountain goats romped in the rolling hills.

Because Israel was such a rich land, many nations were always fighting for it and trying to make it their own.

There came a time 2,000 years ago when the Jews were driven from their beloved land. Soon after this, the wells began to dry up and the dams began to crack and crumble. The hot sands blew over the fields, the vineyards, and the pastures. The land became a useless desert.

But the Jews do not give up easily. Many years later, in 1890, the pioneers ("chalutzim") started returning to Israel. They knew they would have many hard years of work to bring this land back to life. But Jews have never minded hard work. The chalutzim built more dams, dug more wells, drained the water from swamps—and the land began to blossom and come to life.

Today the modern State of Israel is a beautiful, fertile place. Once again golden oranges hang from the trees and huge clusters of grapes hang from the vines.

The Israelis are now more skilled as farmers than ever before. The Israeli government sends farm experts to poorer countries. These experts from Israel live with the people and teach them better ways to farm. Thus Israel shares with its fellow nations and helps make the world a better and more beautiful place in which to live.

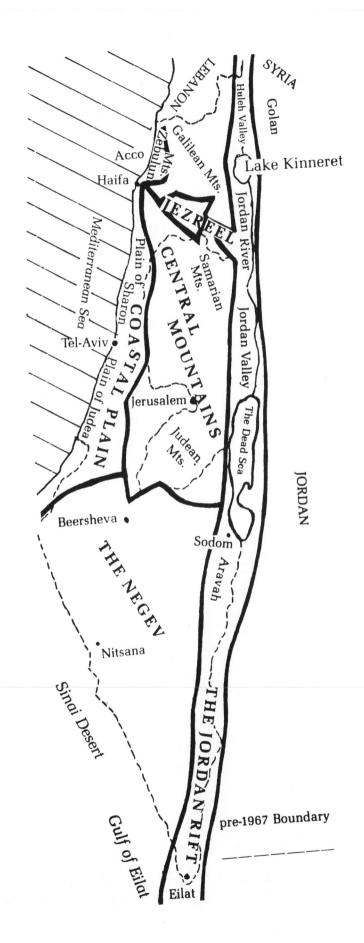

131

The Waters of Meribah

"WATER! GIVE US water!" cried the Children of Israel.

Moses' heart was heavy as he heard his people crying for water. For forty years, this brave leader had led the Children of Israel through the wilderness. Many of the people had grown old and died. Now their sons and daughters were seeking the Promised Land. Moses, too, was growing old and tired. His sister Miriam had died and he was filled with grief. Now the tents of Israel were set up in the Desert of Zin. The streams had all been dried up by the burning sun. There was no water to drink anywhere.

"Better for us if we had died when our mothers and fathers died," cried some of the people to Moses. "Why have you led us into this desert where no seed will grow? Our cattle are dying of thirst!"

Moses and Aaron went into the tabernacle and stood before the altar.

"Show me where to find water for my people," prayed Moses.

"Take thy rod in thy hand," said God, "and lead the people to a rock which I will show you. Speak to the rock and water will pour forth from it."

Moses called the people together and told them to follow him into the desert. As he led them, he heard them grumbling to each other. Suddenly, Moses became very angry. When they came to a large rock, Moses struck it with his rod and cried:

"Give us water!"

The Children of Israel shouted with joy.

Out of the rock came pouring a stream of clear, cold water. The people splashed the water on their hands and faces. The children laughed with glee and danced about in the puddles.

Again God spoke to Moses and said: again:

"I told you to speak to the rock," said God. "But instead you struck it in anger. You did not obey my command. Because of this, you and your brother Aaron will not go into the Promised Land with your people."

Moses bowed his head and wept. He loved the Children of Israel dearly. Now he knew he would soon die and never lead them into their Promised Land.

The place where Moses struck the rock was called Meribah which means "quarrel". For, it was there that the Children of Israel grumbled and quarreled.

CHOOSE THE CORRECT ANSWER.

1. For _____ years Moses had led the Children of Israel through the desert.

2. _____ was the sister of Moses.

3. The tents of Israel were set up in the _____ of Zin.

4. "Speak to the _____ and water will pour forth from it."

5. Out of the rock came pouring forth a stream of clear, cold _____.

6. "You and your brother _____ will not go into the Promised Land."

Aaron , Miriam, desert, rock, water, forty

WHO SAID IT? CHOOSE THE CORRECT ANSWER.

1. "Give us water." _____

2. "Show me where to find water for my people." _____

3. "Take thy rod in thy hand." _____

4. "You and your brother will not go into the Promised Land."

_____

God, Moses, God, Children of Israel

WHY did God punish Moses for striking the rock?
BECAUSE God told Moses to speak to the rock, but instead he struck the rock in anger.

Leaders are specially chosen people who are responsible for their people, their country, or even their companies.

All their actions should be planned beforehand, and they should act with calmness. When you lose your temper you cannot act intelligently.

WHAT'S YOUR TEMPER-ature

Moses lost his temper and instead of speaking to the rock he struck it.

When a child gets upset and angry it doesn't know any better and screams for attention. As the child grows up it learns to control its temper. It is not easy to control one's temper but it can be done if you use your head and work at it. The Torah and the Talmud talk about anger.

Here are three quotations:

"An angry person does stupid things."

"Do not argue with an angry person."

A scholar, if he becomes angry, his wisdom leaves him."

Of course, not all anger is stupid. It is okay to get angry when you see someone mistreating an animal. Or a bully beating up a little kid. Or, someone making fun of an old person. It is also okay to get angry at criminals and at prejudice.

WHAT'S YOUR TEMPER-ature
Answer each question by circling the answer that you think you would do.

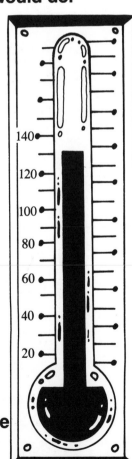

1. You lose your Tzedakah money. Do you:
   a. Kick a rock.
   b. Borrow some money from a friend?
2. You are late for school. Do you:
   a. Lie and make up an excuse.
   b. Say you are sorry and explain what happened?
3. You drop your homework in the mud. Do you:
   a. Copy it over?
   b. Rip it up?
4. You lose the tennis game. Do you:
   a. Shout at the referee for making wrong calls?
   b. Congratulate the other player?

To find your TEMPER-ature use the chart. Find and add the number of points for each question. Discover your TEMPER-ature rating.

1. a. equals 0   b. equals 20   3. a. equals 20   b. equals 0
2. a. equals 0   b. equals 20   4. a. equals 0   b. equals 20

135

Death of Moses

MOSES STOOD IN the doorway of his tent. In the distance he could see the waters of the River Jordan. Beyond the river lay the green fields of the Promised Land. God had told Moses he would never cross the river and enter that wonderful country. But Moses was happy, for he had lived a long life. He had led his people through many dangers. He had taught them the laws of God. Now it was time to choose a new leader for Israel.

Moses called Joshua into his tent and said:

"Soon I will be at rest with my fathers. After I die, you must lead the Children of Israel into the Promised Land."

"But you are still strong and well!" cried Joshua. "How can I take your place as leader?"

"You must not fear," said Moses. "God will be with you always. Now go and tell the people to gather before my tent tomorrow."

The next morning, the Children of Israel stood before their leader. Their hearts were sad, for they knew he was going to speak to them for the last time.

Then Moses blessed the tribes of Israel and sang a beautiful song to them.

"Happy art thou, O Israel," he sang. "Who is like unto thee, O people saved by the Lord. Fear not, for the Lord thy God is with thee. He will not fail thee nor forsake thee."

"Be strong and of good courage, for you will bring the Children of Israel into the land."

Then Moses went up to the top of Mount Nebo. He looked down at the green valley below.

And Moses heard the voice of God saying:

"This is the land which I promised Abraham and Isaac and Jacob. This is the land that shall belong to your children."

Moses died somewhere in the Land of Moab. No person has ever seen his grave. But no man has ever forgotten his name. He was the greatest of all prophets.

The Children of Israel wept and mourned for thirty days after the death of Moses. They knew in their hearts they would never have another leader as great as he had been, or as kind.

CHOOSE THE CORRECT ANSWER.

1. The Israelites reached Canaan

_____.

    a. one year after leaving Egypt

    b. after wandering in the desert
       for forty years

    c. after receiving the Ten
       Commandments

2. Before he died, Moses saw the
land of Canaan from

_____.

    a. Mount Nebo

    b. Mount Sinai

    c. Mount Everest

3. After Moses died

_____ became the

leader.

    a. Aaron

    b. Noah

    c. Joshua

4. Moses was not allowed to enter
the Promised Land because

_____.

    a. he was too old

    b. he had not been a good leader

    c. he had disobeyed God by
       striking the rock

MATCH THE COLUMNS.

1. Land of   Jacob

2. Children of   Land

3. Promised   River

4. Jordan   Moab

5. Abraham, Isaac, and   Israel

WHY did Moses choose Joshua to lead the Israelites into the Land of Canaan?

BECAUSE Moses saw that Joshua was a brave soldier and would make a good leader. After all, it was Joshua who had a mind of his own and could not be influenced by others. Ten of the scouts who entered Canaan were cowards. It was only Joshua and Caleb who were not frightened by the city walls and the fierce words. They believed in God's promise.

The Israelites needed a brave leader, and Joshua was the right choice. When Moses appointed Joshua, it was like one candle passing the light on to another.

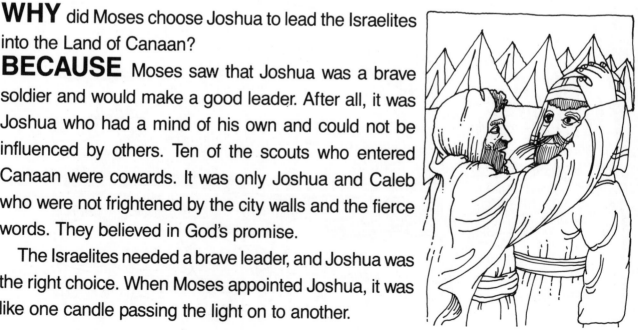

LEADERS OF ISRAEL

Four leaders and soldiers who helped establish the State of Israel.

CHAIM WEIZMANN 1874–1952

Chaim Weizmann was born in Russia. He left in 1892 to study biochemistry in Germany. In 1896, he heard Theodor Herzl speak. Deeply inspired, he joined the Zionist movement.

Weizmann was a talented scientist and expert on acetone, a substance used in making explosives.

When World War I began, Winston Churchill sent for Chaim Weizmann. Britain needed explosives for the war. He asked the chemist to produce 30,000 gallons of acetone. In appreciation for his help, the Jews were allowed to settle in Palestine and build a homeland there.

Weizmann was an active Zionist leader, raising funds to save Jewish refugees and Holocaust survivors and to establish a scientific institute in Israel. When the State of Israel was established in 1948, he was elected its first President.

After he died, the scientific institute was named the Weizmann Institute of Science.

HANNAH SENESH 1921–1944

Hannah Senesh grew up in Hungary and settled in Israel at the age of eighteen. During World War II she volunteered to help rescue Hungarian Jews from the Nazis. She was parachuted into Italy, made her way to Yugoslavia, and then tried to enter Hungary. At the Hungarian border she was captured by police.

The girl was cruelly tortured and beaten in the Nazi effort to force her to reveal information about Jewish underground activities. But the brave girl remained silent. The Hungarian police shot her dead in November 1944.

In 1950, Hannah Senesh's remains were brought to Israel and buried on Mount Herzl. In Israel and among Jews everywhere, her name became a symbol of devotion and self-sacrifice.

DAVID MARCUS 1902–1948

Born and raised in Brooklyn, David Marcus studied at the United States Military Academy at West Point.

During World War II, Marcus fought bravely and advanced to the rank of colonel.

Marcus returned to New York and opened a law office in January 1948. That same month, an Israeli Haganah member, Shlomo Shamir, came to the United States and approached Marcus for help: "You have studied military tactics at West Point, and you can help us build our strength in Palestine. Please help us."

Marcus left for Palestine the same month. Smuggled into Tel Aviv as Michael Stone, he led Haganah raids and helped plan Israel's future defense.

Two weeks after Israel was proclaimed a state, Prime Minister Ben-Gurion appointed David Marcus the commander of the Jerusalem front. Thanks to Marcus's efforts, the Jewish forces saved Jerusalem's new city from the enemy. But David Marcus was killed in the fighting.

ELI COHEN 1924–1965

Born in Egypt, Eli Cohen learned the language and customs of the Arabs while he was growing up. Later he moved to Israel and trained to become a spy. He was sent to Syria, where he pretended to be a rich Syrian citizen, using an Arabic name.

Cohen was very successful in his daring work for Israeli intelligence. He became friendly with top government officials, who told him important secrets. He was taken on tours of hidden Syrian army bases. He was able to help the Israeli government and army with this important information.

Cohen fit so well into Arab society that he began his own show on Syrian radio and became well known through the entire nation. In 1965 he was caught by the Syrians and hanged.